Theodore Frelinghuysen Seward

The School of Life

Divine Providence in the Light of Modern Science

Theodore Frelinghuysen Seward

The School of Life
Divine Providence in the Light of Modern Science

ISBN/EAN: 9783337253196

Printed in Europe, USA, Canada, Australia, Japan

Cover: Foto ©Lupo / pixelio.de

More available books at **www.hansebooks.com**

THE SCHOOL OF LIFE

DIVINE PROVIDENCE IN THE LIGHT OF
MODERN SCIENCE
THE LAW OF DEVELOPMENT APPLIED TO CHRISTIAN
THINKING AND CHRISTIAN LIVING

BY

THEODORE F. SEWARD

"Religion and Science, by virtue of their affinity, will one day meet, and the world will get what it needs and cries for — not a new religion, but the revelation of Revelation."
COUNT DE MAISTRE.

"The doctrine of evolution stands to-day for the scientific view of life, and the more that view can be brought home to the masses, the surer will be the foundations of the state, and the more rapidly and happily will the stages that yet separate us from a condition of perfect social health be accomplished."
POPULAR SCIENCE MONTHLY.

NEW YORK
JAMES POTT & CO. PUBLISHERS
114 Fifth Avenue
LONDON
S. BAGSTER & SONS LIMITED
1895

We naturally desire to do, while it is God's plan that we shall be. Yet we must be in our doing. What, then, shall we do in order to secure the best being? What God wants us to do. This is the whole philosophy of eternal life. It is the lesson we are sent into this world to learn.

---

*Fate frowned upon me in my thoughtless youth:
I shrank in fear, I trembled 'neath the rod;
But life hath taught me well this deeper truth,
The frowns of fate are but the smiles of God.*

Press of A. G. SHERWOOD & CO.
New York

PREFACE.

"THE beginning and the end of what is the matter with us in these days," says Carlyle, "is that we have forgotten God." In what sense can this be true? The air has never been so full of theology—God-talk—as it is now.

What we have forgotten, or are in danger of forgetting, is not the truth that there is a God, but the nature of his relation to us. The vast increase of scientific knowledge at the present day has, for the moment, a confusing tendency. "All things are governed by law," we are told; and the inference seems inevitable—" then they cannot be governed by God," and our faith in Divine Providence is rudely shaken.

A deeper study of the subject not only restores our faith, but shows that science has given a new foundation for it. In proving the universality of law, science confirms the doctrine of the omnipresence of God. "Atheism is very bad metaphysics," says Professor John Fiske. But the truth has not yet come home to the heart of Christendom with all its comforting conviction that the God revealed by science is just the perfect Heavenly Father that the Bible declares him to be. The external God of medieval theology may be an arbitrary Being, but the "immanent God" revealed by Jesus Christ, whose ways in the universe are now shown by the investigations of science, cannot be separated from his creatures for an instant. "To those who believe in God the most minute natural phenomena must be divine. I say deliberately, divine. The grain of dust is a thought of God. God's power made it. God's wisdom gave it whatsoever properties or qualities it may possess. God's providence has put it in the place where it is now, and has ordained that it should be in that place at this moment by a train of causes and effects which reaches back to the very creation of the universe. The grain of dust can no more go from God's presence or flee from his Spirit than you or I can."[1]

It is true that God is a Being of law. All laws emanate from him. He lives in his laws. He gives through his laws. He controls the universe and the affairs of men by his laws. Yet in all these manifestations of law he is a loving Father adapting his care with infinite minuteness to the special needs of every individual.

The theory of the divine immanence brings us face to face with an unavoidable issue. It creates an alternative which we cannot escape. God must either be in all things or in nothing. His providence must either be universal or void. He either governs the universe in the smallest particulars, or he surrenders it wholly to a general law separate from himself. The Christian believer cannot for a moment allow the possibility of the latter alternative; yet the full and practical acceptance of the former is not easy. To recognize God beneath his laws, and to believe that he controls them with reference to the welfare of each individual, is, indeed, a test of faith. It has an appearance of fatalism. But it is as distinct from fatalism

[1] Charles Kingsley.

as a spurious coin is from the genuine. Fatalism is blind and ignorant. Faith is intelligent and far-seeing. Intelligent faith says, Although I cannot fathom the process, I know that, as all things subsist from God, and as God is infinite, his plan must include all things. As my freedom of action is one of the " all things," his plan must include my freedom of action. In other words, while I choose, decide, and act in the free and unrestrained exercise of my will, God's plan is at the same time being carried out through my choosing, deciding, and acting.

All Christians profess to believe in Divine Providence, but the belief of many is like a chain of which the central link has a fatal weakness. They believe in a general Providence, but deny or doubt its application to particulars. This is a palpable absurdity. It has always been a logical absurdity. The recognition of an immanent or indwelling God reduces it to a scientific absurdity. The practical unbelief of the Christian church in Divine Providence is the foundation of its weaknesses and shortcomings. When that question is properly settled, all other questions will be settled. If we really believe that God has a plan for our life, we will give up planning for selfish purposes, and will seek from day to day to enter into God's infinite designs, or will try to adjust our plan to his higher overruling purpose. Doubting that, we can only act as most of us do—work and strive and worry as if our Heavenly Father had no interest, or only a very remote interest, in our welfare. Our chief aim, and the motive-power behind our desperate struggles, is the desire (shall we not confess it?) to become independent of God. We can be at rest in our minds when we have a competent fortune, or a good paying business, or an assured income from any source, but if we have only our Heavenly Father to depend upon we are the prey of endless doubts and fears. In this respect our faith is of little more value than a pagan's faith.

The time must come when a belief in Divine Providence—a full and practical belief—will be the supreme test of discipleship. Such a faith is an inevitable corollary of the proposition that God is within the universe and in no possible or conceivable sense outside of it. This was the teaching of our Saviour, and science now confirms it. The materialist can justly say: "We carry our belief in a resident force to a consistent application, and accept the logical outcome of our premises without shrinking. You claim this inherent force to be the direct act of a Supreme Being, but you do not pretend to go where your logic carries you." This criticism is just, and it must be met. The church has a very slight hold upon the masses of the people. Why? Because the people see that the votaries of religion are, as a rule, as much in bondage to the world and its methods as they are themselves. A sailor, seeing a clergyman trembling with fear during a storm, said to his comrades, "The preacher is as much afraid of going to heaven as we are of going to hell." And not only in times of danger, but in the ordinary routine of life, the world sees but little evidence among Christians of an actual belief in a Heavenly Father's care. Hence they are practical agnostics. "How can we know there is a God?" they say. "We cannot see him nor hear him speak, and when we look at the people who profess to believe in him, we find little evidence of it in their lives. They have a book which (as they say) tells about him and gives instructions concerning this world and the next, but very few of them live up to its teachings, or even try to, as far as we can see."

This is a severe indictment, but who can say that it is unjust? There is only one way to meet it: our theoretical faith must be exchanged for a practical faith. Having found a scientific basis for a belief in the universality of Divine Providence, it becomes the duty of the Christian church to proclaim it anew, and to live in accordance with it. If science, with its revelations of the law of development and its suggestions of immortality, shows this life to be a period of preparation, then it is not only unwise but unscientific to live wholly or chiefly for the things of time and sense.

Being deeply impressed with the need of a new presentation of the subject of Divine Providence in the light of modern science, I offer this book to the public in the hope that it may not only increase the faith of the Christian reader in our Heavenly Father's care, but that it may also give a helpful direction to the thought and life of those who are dissatisfied with the old theological statements but have not yet found a substitute upon which they are contented to rest. The feeling of many of this class is voiced in these pathetic words of an avowed agnostic: " In my opinion, while materialism is better than orthodox Christianity—better because it is preferable to be annihilated than to run the chance of going to a horrible hell or a gingerbread heaven—it is nevertheless a cheerless belief that takes all the meaning out of life. With my present knowledge I am forced into materialism, but I abhor the idea that dirt I am and to dirt I must return, and would be very thankful to have some facts upon which to ground a more cheerful belief."

The doctrine of an immanent God, or what is now known as Christian evolution, affords all the ground that is needed for "a more cheerful belief." It shows this world's history to be not the melancholy record of a dismal failure, but the normal development of an orderly plan. It is a key to all problems, whether material or spiritual. It embodies the entire philosophy of education, and indicates the lines upon which the educative process should be carried out. He who would be truly wise must study the laws of relation, for in those laws will be found the basis of all knowledge. They may be classified as follows:

1. The relation of the Creator to the universe.
2. The relation of the Heavenly Father to the human race, his children.
3. The relation of man to his brother.
4. The relation of the spiritual to the material.
5. The relation of conduct to character.
6. The relation of character to destiny.

All that is written in the following pages has reference to one or more of these laws, not as matter of theory alone, but as the outgrowth of experience. It may truly be said that this is not so much a book that has been written as one that has written itself. I may go still further and say that it is not so much a book as a life, and therefore I indulge the hope that it may exercise some degree of helpful influence upon other lives.

THEODORE F. SEWARD.

CONTENTS.

	PAGE
INTRODUCTION	1

CHAPTER I.
THE SCRIPTURAL DOCTRINE OF A UNIVERSAL PROVIDENCE CONFIRMED BY MODERN SCIENCE 10

CHAPTER II.
HOW THE SCHOOL-HOUSE WAS BUILT—A PANORAMA OF CREATION .. 20

CHAPTER III.
WHY THE SCHOOL-HOUSE WAS BUILT—THE PURPOSE OF CREATION .. 32

CHAPTER IV.
A HUMAN GOD AND A HUMANE FATHER—A REASONABLE ANTHROPOMORPHISM 42

CHAPTER V.
WHERE IS GOD? 48

CHAPTER VI.
THE PROVIDENTIAL RELATION OF INDIVIDUALS TO HISTORIC EVENTS 59

CHAPTER VII.
A DIVINE PLAN FOR EVERY LIFE 65

CHAPTER VIII.
DIFFICULTIES CLASSIFIED AND CONSIDERED 74

CHAPTER IX.

Our Father's Plan for Each and All, Including............ 87
    Heredity,   Health,
    Early environment,   Usefulness,
    Education,   Living martyrdom,
    Occupation or Business,   Marriage,
    Success,   Duration of life.
    Money,

CHAPTER X.

A Rational Heaven.. 110

CHAPTER XI.

The Great Insanity—Living for this World................ 126

CHAPTER XII.

Our Schoolmasters—Uncertainty, Suffering, Death, Catastrophe, Nature 132

CHAPTER XIII.

Our Course of Study.. 142

CHAPTER XIV.

Spiritual Alchemy, or the Law of Growth 147

CHAPTER XV.

Spiritual Growth an Unconscious Process 156

CHAPTER XVI.

Prayer in its Relation to a Universal Providence......... 160

CHAPTER XVII.

To what Extent are we Responsible for Others?........... 168

CHAPTER XVIII.

Some Dark Problems.. 172
    The cruelty of Nature's laws.
    Suffering among animals.
    The sufferings of children.
    Poverty of the masses.
    The fate of the heathen.
    Public calamities.
    General remarks concerning dark problems.

CHAPTER XIX.

Short Talks on Vital Topics 194
    Are we pilgrims or tramps?
    The two doctrinal hemispheres: God's sovereignty and man's free agency.
    Working with God.
    What is conversion?
    The kingdom within.
    The stupidity of ingratitude.
    What must the Christian do to be saved?
    Heavenly conversation.
    Atmospheric religion, or spiritual radiation.
    Spiritual law in the natural world.
    The Lord Jesus Christ as an evolutionist.

CHAPTER XX.

Evolution and the Christian Doctrines 226
    Evolution and the Bible.   Evolution and foreordination.
    Evolution and the Fall.   Evolution and the Trinity.
    Evolution and total depravity.   Evolution and the Atonement.
        The testimony of Science.

CHAPTER XXI.

The Ways of God in this New Age........................ 253

THE SCHOOL OF LIFE.

INTRODUCTION.

THE present age is very commonly characterized as materialistic. On the contrary, it possesses elements of spirituality beyond any age that has preceded it. The error arises from mistaking a mere passing experience for a permanent quality, a tidal wave on the surface of the ocean for the ocean itself. It is true that a spasm of materialism followed the first promulgation of the theory of evolution. The apostles of matter took the subject into their own hands and proceeded to instruct the world that "the molten earth contained within it elements of life which grouped themselves into their present forms as the planet cooled." For a time it was considered the proper thing to deny all supernatural agency, and to regard matter as sufficient unto itself. There were some who even persuaded themselves that they were willing at the end of life "to melt like streaks of morning cloud into the infinite azure of the past."[1] Immortality was not personal, but merely an influence bequeathed to succeeding generations. "As we live for others in life, so do we live in

[1] Professor Tyndall.

others after death. . . . How deeply does such a belief as this bring home to each moment of life the mysterious perpetuity of ourselves!"[1]

But the reign of the materialist was short. A host of Christian teachers arose whose scientific equipment was fully equal to that of the enemies of our faith, with a wisdom which enabled them to see and acknowledge the evidences of a Higher Law within and above the substances of the material world. As a test of the spiritual quality of this age it is enough to ask the question, Where are the infidels of the past? The race is nearly extinct. In place of infidelity we have the far milder and more modest protest of the agnostic. Instead of "There is no God, no immortal life," we hear only words of doubt. "We do not know, we cannot tell." This, also, is a passing phase. Honest doubt is in reality a form of interrogation, and when a human soul begins to ask for the truth, the blessed revelation is not far away. Thus we see that the man who has been regarded as the apostle of agnosticism, Herbert Spencer, has so far passed beyond the quicksands of doubt as to become convinced that, to use his own language, "we are ever in the presence of an Infinite and Eternal Energy from which all things proceed."

The time is rapidly approaching when the presence of an unseen God in the universe will be accepted on the same ground as the presence of an unseen soul in man. The latter cannot be proved by a mathematical demonstration, nor by the rules of logic. We judge man to have a soul by what it does in and through the body. By a parity of reasoning we must judge that the universe has a soul. We see the same evidence in the universe as in the human

[1] Frederick Harrison.

body of a Will working in and through it, a conscious Being who feels, loves, plans, and executes.

How can we do otherwise than describe as a spiritual age the era in which the truth breaks in upon the consciousness of the race that what have been regarded as material forces are really spiritual forces; when it even begins to be surmised that matter itself has a spiritual origin? It is a day of wonderful revelations and strange reconciliations. The most significant of these reconciliations, that which in a sense includes all others, is the new and thrice-blessed union and fellowship of science and religion. Theology has heretofore looked upon science as an enemy of religion; as if religion were a tender lamb, and science a fierce wolf ready and anxious to pounce upon it and destroy it. How rapidly is this feeling passing away! It would not fully express the truth to say that the former antagonism has disappeared. In place of antagonism and fear has come a recognition of the truth that science is furnishing the most effective arguments and weapons of defense the Christian faith has ever gained outside of the sacred Scriptures. That all scientists and all friends of Christianity do not yet realize this in no wise affects the truth itself. That some do not yet see the laws of nature as the laws of God proves nothing but the limitation of their own vision. They are shut in by a self-created horizon.

In substituting an immanent God for an external God science has rendered a supreme service to mankind. It gives a basis of order and system in the moral world, as the theory of Copernicus gave order and system in the physical universe. It marks the beginning of a new epoch in the religious history of the race as truly as the Copernican theory revolutionized astronomy. In point of fact, the great religious movement of the new age was initiated by science and not by theology. Copernicus was as necessary a forerunner of Calvin and Luther as of Kepler and Newton. A correct idea of the physical universe was essential to a true conception of God in the universe. The progress of science since that time has been gradual, but no more so than the evolution of religious thought. Neither Copernicus nor Calvin spoke the final word. The former revealed to mankind an orderly universe. The latter exalted God as its Sovereign Ruler. If Calvin's God appears to us too arbitrary, it must be remembered that he only reflected the spirit of the times in which he lived and wrought. No other conception would have suited that rude and tyrannical age. Since that period religion and science have worked side by side at the great problem of Divine Providence, or God's relation to his creation and his creatures. Although apparently antagonistic, they were, in reality, working toward the same end, each having a different but equally essential phase of the problem to solve.

At last the point is reached when the great truth is revealed that God has not given one revelation of himself in nature and another and different revelation in the Bible. They are counterparts of each other. The apparent inconsistency and antagonism arose wholly from our imperfect knowledge. We judged from appearances, and appearances are often deceptive. Our Lord's injunction, " Judge not according to the appearance, but judge righteous judgment," has a wider application than we supposed.

Science loses nothing, but gains infinitely, by her recognition of God as the Author of matter and the direct

Source of its forces or laws. When it was decided that the first message to be sent by telegraph should be the words "What hath God wrought!" it seemed a happy inspiration. It was much more than that. It was typical. It was a prophecy of the new day, just dawning, when science should add to all her other glories that of acknowledging the Divine Source of nature's phenomena. By this acknowledgment and all that is involved in it, science ceases to be science merely, and takes its place among the active religious forces of our time. The Bible tells us to consider the lily and the mustard-seed, and study the law of growth in them. Science now brings us the same message and bids us consider the ways of God in the marvelous processes of nature. What we find is thus eloquently described by a reverent observer:[1]

"Take a grain of corn and make a thin transverse section of it and place it under your microscope. It is vegetable fiber, arranged symmetrically. And that is all you see. Take another seed of the same kind and put it in the soil. You have not discovered any resident force in the section under your microscope, but you know it is there; and it begins to act when placed in suitable conditions. It acts as chemist, making wisest choice of fit substance for its purpose; it acts as master-builder, marshaling its multitude of servants; it acts as architect, giving proportion and form to the uprising structure; it acts as engineer, pumping water to every part; it is a whole municipal board, attending to a million details, from the subways where its roots are pushed to reach their supplies, up to

---

[1] Rev. Myron Adams, of Plymouth Church, Rochester, N. Y. Although he speaks of "resident force," the whole purpose of his argument is to show that it is only God's method of operation.

the tassels and spires which rise like minarets over the whole corporate structure. I may seem to the reader to be talking in a strain of extravagant diction, trying to spread a web of words over a very small thing, namely, a grain of corn; but I assure you it is so far out of my power to do any fraction of justice to the subject that I feel discouraged at the start. The resident force in a grain of corn is of so intricate, so subtle, so skilful, so altogether wonderful a character, that it can be spoken of only in a way of feeble comparison with our own chemical, architectural, and other proceedings which it throws far into the shade."

There is one historical fact which has not thus far received a due share of attention. It is this: *Spiritual evolution was given to the world before material evolution was dreamed of.*

It may be truly claimed that our Lord himself announced the evolutionary principle when he said, "The kingdom of God is within you," and proceeded to describe the law of growth—"first the blade, then the ear, after that the full corn in the ear." But the principle required to be unfolded, to be more fully stated, and especially to be practically applied to the needs of humanity. This great work was begun by Frederick Froebel. He saw the infinite depth of the Saviour's declarations, "A little child shall lead them," "Except ye become as little children ye cannot enter into the kingdom of heaven." Froebel inaugurated a new era in human history by the enunciation of the following maxim, " Union of the soul with God is the end and aim of all true education." In the application of this principle he began at the only proper point—the dawning consciousness of the child. He showed how its plays could and should be made the foundation of all its future development. His school is a child-garden, where the innate powers are to be fostered, developed, and trained. His first gift to the child is a sphere, which represents the earth and all the heavenly bodies. The second gift is a cube, representing the mineral kingdom. The third, a cylinder, suggests the various forms of the vegetable and animal worlds. Thus, when scarcely out of its mother's arms, the child is inducted into the fundamental principles of all its future knowledge. The methods of the kindergarten are found to be necessary at each step of progress, and are therefore carried into the primary school, the grammar school, the college, the university. In truth, as the laws of growth are uniform and eternal, it is beyond question that Froebel introduced into the world an educational process which is to be continued through all eternity.

The transforming power of the principle of evolution as revealing the methods of an immanent God is literally beyond our comprehension. It effects a complete reversal of human standards. It changes the standard from the intellectual to the moral. It introduces an era in which a man's character will no more be judged by his intellect than by his muscles. The intellect, like the hand, is only a tool to work with. That which makes or unmakes the man is the motive with which he uses his intellect, his hand, his wealth-producing faculty, his moral nature, or any other gifts with which God has endowed him. It settles the old vexed question of morality. It has been common in the church to treat morality as a deadly sin. Anathemas have been hurled against the moralist, as if he were the worst, because the most subtle, enemy of religion. That depends. It is purely a question of motives. If he uses morality for selfish ends, he is building a hell in his own soul instead of a heaven. If he uses it for his fellow-men, he is developing the heavenly principle in his own being, though he may not be aware of it.

But all this is as true of the religionist as of the moralist. It is an amazing fact that the church has for eighteen hundred years made the profession of a belief *about* Christ the standard of its membership, when he took the utmost pains to forestall that error. He carefully explained, with many reiterations, that the sole test of Christian character is loving service—denying self for the good of others. He even went so far as to give a minute and graphic description of the disappointment and discomfiture of those who count themselves his friends yet fail to obey his precepts. "Depart from me. I never knew you." He made it clear that the Christian has but one vocation—to love; and that his worldly business or profession should be an avocation; not a means of self-aggrandizement, but purely a medium of service to his fellow-men.

The "divine immanence" hypothesis changes our conception of God from an arbitrary monarch upon a throne to a benign sun in the heavens. The former analogy was suited to the past condition of the race. It was the basis of all the medieval creeds and "confessions," but is not a working hypothesis in the vastly increased knowledge and enlightenment of the present day. Under the first figure, all men were born as aliens, enemies of God, children of Satan. Becoming a Christian was deserting the cohorts of hell and joining the army of heaven. Under the new figure (which is as truly scriptural as the first) all people are creations of God just as all plants are creations of the sun. This truth shows that the whole of life is an education, and that all education is religious—that is, it has a bearing upon the eternal destiny of the individual. As the character of any form of growth in the vegetable kingdom is determined by the use it makes of the sunlight, so the character of a human being is determined by the use he makes of the divine life. The plant may turn the sunlight into poison, and man may pervert the divine life to selfishness and unrighteousness. But the latter process is not a *lack* of education, it is an *evil* education—a training downward instead of upward. In the light of this truth the earth is seen to be a school-room; its facts and phenomena are the school apparatus, devised and used for our education; God himself is the Teacher, and life is from beginning to end a course of moral and religious training. The idea that the business of the school-teacher is to train the intellectual powers merely, and that his graduates are afterward to be taken in hand by the clergyman, to be "converted" and taught religion, is exploded forever. Education in its true sense is religion, and religion is education. If the divine life is not received, the selfish principle will grow.

Divine Providence, as related to the human race, is God's method of educating it.

CHAPTER I.

THE SCRIPTURAL DOCTRINE OF A UNIVERSAL PROVIDENCE CONFIRMED BY MODERN SCIENCE.

NOTE.—In many minds there still remains in connection with the theory of evolution some degree of the misapprehension which was created by the imperfect and misleading method of its original promulgation. For the benefit of readers who have not thoroughly investigated the subject it should be stated that the term properly refers only to a *process*. Webster defines evolution as " the act of unfolding or unrolling; hence, in the process of growth, development, as the *evolution* of a flower from a bud, or an animal from the egg." It will thus be seen that evolution is no more opposed to Christianity than gravitation or any other law of nature.

The question as to the source of evolution, or the power behind it, is wholly distinct from the method itself. As there are some who believe and teach that this power is inherent in the material atoms, the term " Christian evolution " is often employed to indicate the theory of a divine origin of the force. It is hardly necessary to say that in this book the term is only used in its Christian sense, always implying that, as Dr. McCosh expresses it, " in this world things are so connected that every one thing proceeds from some other, and all things from God." This law applies not only to the physical or material world, but equally to mental and spiritual phenomena.

HUMAN thought and human life—individual and social—are now undergoing a process of transformation. The underlying principle of the change is indicated by the expression " an immanent God." Although this is a theological term, yet, strange to say, its explanation is not to be found in the instructions of theology, but of science.

An immanent God is a Supreme Being who works from within. How? Theology cannot tell. But science steps forward, and reveals a process which the Christian believer, as soon as he understands it, accepts joyfully as the divine method. It is true that all the details are not yet made clear, but the revelations are now on so vast a scale that the unknown may fairly be inferred. The scientific theory has established itself as a satisfactory solution of the problem of the material universe—its nature and the method of its construction. The process is explained by the name given to it—evolution, an unfolding, a growth or development from within.

The various lines upon which science is conducting her experiments and investigations are rapidly converging toward one stupendous conclusion, namely, that all substances, all forces, all laws, are reducible to a single element or unit; that the material universe is uniform in substance throughout its vast immensity, and that light, heat, sound, electricity, chemical affinity, attraction, are only varied manifestations of one and the same force. More than this, it is being widely conceded by many of the deepest thinkers that the unknown " something " toward which the revelations of science point as the basis of matter is not material, but spiritual. Faraday speaks of the original atom as " a point of force." Morell says: " Matter, after all, may be reduced to force, and force to spirit as its source and spring." Delsarte says: " All things visible are the expression of an interior spiritual essence." Oersted says: " The conception of the universe is incomplete if not comprehended as the constant and continuous work of the eternally creating Spirit." The authors of " The Unseen Universe " prove, by a line of argument that has never been controverted, that the visible universe is developed from the invisible. Joseph Cook says: " As science progresses, it draws nearer in all its forms to the proof of the spiritual origin of force—that is, of the divine immanence in natural law." Carlyle says: "Matter exists only spiritually, and to represent some idea and body it forth." Even Darwin said: "I am willing to admit that the ultimate cause beyond all motion is immaterial—that is to say, God."

The primal germ of life is found to be the same in all plants, animals, insects; in the worm that crawls and the bird that flies; in the sting of the bee and the brain of the naturalist who studies it. Huxley calls it "the clay of the potter." After witnessing the development of animal life from the protoplasm by the aid of his microscope, he says: "After watching the process hour by hour one is almost involuntarily possessed by the notion that some more subtle aid to vision than an achromatic would show the hidden artist, with his plan before him, striving with skilful manipulation to perfect his work."

This is the testimony of the scientist, pure and simple, judging only from what he sees with his natural vision. Devout Christians are wont to be disturbed because he stops at this point and fails to acknowledge the Divine Source of the power he so eloquently describes. The criticism is wholly out of place. The anxiety is wasted. The scientist, as a scientist, should not be swayed by theory in his investigations. If he is a Christian as well as a scientist, he may rejoice in the new evidence he has found in the revelations of the microscope, or "the testimony of the rocks," as to the wisdom and goodness of the God he worships. But this he does as a Christian and not as a scientist. There have been many cases in which the work of scientific men has been hindered by their theological bias. Leibnitz, whose genius was scarcely inferior to that of

Newton, refused to accept the latter's theory of gravitation because it seemed to substitute a lower force for the direct power of God. Agassiz was deterred by similar considerations from adopting the theory of evolution, although his magnificent contributions to the sum of scientific knowledge gave it, unconsciously to himself, a valuable support.

The changed relation of science to religion has no more striking illustration than in the fact that the former can now be called upon to bear testimony to the doctrine of Universal Providence—testimony of such a character as to stand side by side with the Word of God. In truth, it should be said that it *is* the Word of God as written in nature.

The appearance of the new witness is most opportune. This is, above all things, a questioning age. Men will no longer accept a "Thus saith the Lord" without some reasonable basis for the theory or the alleged truth for which their credence is demanded. This is not a change to be deplored, it is rather an occasion for thankfulness, as indicating the higher level our race has attained in its upward progress. An unquestioning faith was necessary while the commonest laws and processes of nature were unknown—a book unopened and unread. But we are now probing the very heart of the universe and bringing forth into the light its deepest mysteries. If a knowledge of these mysteries will not only enlarge and dignify our conception of the material creation, revealing order and method where chaos and confusion appeared to reign; if, in addition to such a result in the world of matter, we can find a law enforcing the doctrine of a Universal Providence, and giving to the humblest Christian a new ground for belief in a divine supervision which will not even allow a sparrow to fall without the Heavenly Father's notice and care, then we may gratefully acknowledge that science, instead of being an enemy of religion, is the best friend and the most important ally our faith has ever gained.

Theology alone cannot satisfactorily account for the divine immanence, and explain its methods, because it is obliged to take the scriptural account of creation literally. It could not do otherwise. It therefore gave a conception of God as separate from the universe and calling all things into existence by a word of command—"shouting Hebrew into space," as one writer expresses it. Carlyle characterizes the idea as that of "an absentee God, sitting idle ever since the first sabbath at the outside of his universe and seeing it go." It has also been aptly called a "carpenter conception" of creation. One writer thus pithily describes the method: "First there was nothing, then there was an elephant." Charles Kingsley describes it as "the theory that God has wound up the universe like a clock and left it to tick by itself till it runs down, only at rare intervals interposing miraculous interferences with the laws which he himself has made."

A mistaken impression of the laws and methods of Divine Providence was an inevitable result of such a theory. Whatever the degree of faith exercised under that conception—and we know that it has often been of the sublimest character—must of necessity have a substratum of error in theory if not in practice. If God's care is that of a Being outside of the universe, then, as human nature is constituted, nothing can wholly banish from our minds the impression that his method must be, as the late Dr. Hodge expressed it, to "come down upon the world at intervals and in spots." That this idea widely prevails is shown by the common use of the term "special providence," as if God had more to do with one event or class of events than another. Even in the pulpit allusions are often made to the "interpositions" of Divine Providence, thus confirming the false impression of help coming from without.

It is not easy to derive consolation or strength from this conception. It is too vague, and too suggestive of an unpleasant alternative. If God's help comes from without, and if his visits are "special," then we have nothing fixed and certain upon which to rest. If he sometimes comes, he may also sometimes stay away. How are we poor, ignorant, and especially we sinful and erring mortals to be certain that this or that is a time of his visitation? There are many reasons for supposing that the present occasion is *not* one of those times. The trouble that is now upon us came largely from our own folly, or perhaps from positive wrong-doing. What right have we to expect that God will interpose and prevent the legitimate consequences of our blunders—still less of our sins?

Such a process of reasoning grows logically out of the idea of an external God. To accept fully the promises of the Bible against this undercurrent of doubt is possible only to a few who are favored with peculiar mental constitutions. Most Christians give up the problem as quite beyond their grasp, and secure what comfort they can from the general promise that "all things shall work together for good," but rarely have the courage to apply the promise to what they call the petty details of life, forgetting that

> There is no great or small
> To the God who maketh all.

By the revelations of science the theory of an external God is banished forever. It can no more be revived than the Ptolemaic system of astronomy. It has no logical basis. It is not in accordance with an enlightened interpretation of the Scriptures. It fails to satisfy either the reason or the heart.

The Christian public have feared to accept the theory of evolution, because it was first advanced from its purely scientific side, and thus appeared to support the claims of materialism. It was to be expected that the materialists would make such a use of it, and for a time they seemed to have it all their own way. But this was only because devout scientists like Agassiz and Sir Charles Lyell misapprehended the subject at the outset, and failed to realize that the *great opportunity* of theism had arrived; that the evolutionists had created a magnificent system, of which the only element lacking was that which the Christian supplies by substituting a Supreme Power, a Divine Creator, for the "resident force" of the materialist.

We must once more remind ourselves that the special province of the scientist is to observe, to investigate, and to record the results of his investigations. If he goes beyond this and deduces theories from his facts, he enters another field—that of the philosopher, or the theologian. This, of course, he has a perfect right to do; but it is no more his privilege to make such use of his facts than it is that of the professional philosopher or theologian. He has no preëmptive claim upon the scientific truths or principles he has brought to light. "It is the duty of the scientist to find out the *how* of things, and of the Christian to find out the *why*."

The question now to be considered is this: What facts,

principles, or processes has science revealed which will aid us in forming a rational conception of God's relation to the universe and to all things contained therein? In briefest outline, the theory which is now most widely accepted by the highest authorities is this: The matter out of which the universe has been created was originally in a highly diffused state, its atoms being infinitely, or at least inconceivably, minute. These atoms, created by God, were the material out of which the future worlds were to be made. By his power (acting in accordance with certain fixed methods which we call laws) the atoms were gathered together in the condition which we describe as "nebulous"; from this they were gradually molded into worlds; by the unceasing exercise of the same power they were held in their proper orbits as they revolved about the central orb; and by this power as a creative force all substances and forms of life were in due time produced. The work thus begun by the Divine Creator is continued in perpetual exercise. He holds in place each revolving atom in a mass of granite. He builds the stately oak. He shapes the queenly rose and the modest violet, and endows them with their exquisite fragrance. In a word, he is the Masterbuilder by whom all things are created and sustained, whether in the heaven above or in the earth beneath or in the waters under the earth.

To the intelligent Christian believer this theory is like a revelation from heaven. Instead of robbing him of his faith it gives him a new foundation for his faith. It introduces an element of rationality into his belief. That which he formerly believed as the Word of God, although apparently contrary to his reason, he may now believe as the Word of God because it is in accordance with his reason.

The theory of "resident force" is a source of deep perplexity to the agnostic scientist, who can find no origin for it. To the Christian it is a solution of all difficulties in the world of matter. The resident force is God, and its so-called laws are his methods of operation. The scriptural declaration that "God so clothes the flower" ceases to be poetical and becomes an accurate scientific statement. The votaries of science may or may not share our faith as to the origin of the force they describe, but there is no reasonable ground upon which they can deny it. If they choose to believe that the original atoms were self-created, and that they had a self-derived ability to "put their heads together and construct the universe," there is no law to prevent it. But to go beyond this and describe their theory as "rational" while they characterize the Christian's belief as "superstition" is a gigantic assumption against which the common sense of mankind has a right to enter a vigorous protest.

The number of scientists who accept "divine immanence" as the only rational theory by which to account for "resident force" is constantly increasing. Professor C. A. Young, the astronomer, when asked to state his opinion regarding the forces which move and control the planets, replied thus in effect: "By the exercise of my will I lift my arm and move my body. I think that it is in some similar way, by the exercise of God's will, that the heavenly bodies are moved and controlled." Herschel said: "It is but reasonable to regard the force of gravitation as the direct result of a consciousness or a will existing somewhere."

The researches of science have given us a God within in place of a God without. They have shown us how his power is exercised in creating all objects, and how it must be continually exerted in sustaining them after they are created. "Preservation is perpetual creation." It shows how he works, not *by* a general law, as if this law were something separate from himself, but in accordance with what we call a law, which is only his method of operation. In a word, the doctrine of Divine Providence has passed from the realm of faith to the realm of science. The Bible teaches us that we have a Heavenly Father. Science confirms this instruction, and reveals our Father's ways of working. Before considering the application of providential laws and methods to the experiences of life, let us in the next chapter review the process by which this world, our temporary home, our school, the scene of our disciplinary and formative experience, was constructed.

CHAPTER II.

HOW THE SCHOOL-HOUSE WAS BUILT.

IF creation was not instantaneous, by what process was the earth constructed? The "fiat" theory is so fixed in our minds by the influence of early instruction and association that it is worth while for readers who have not made a special study of the subject to consider for a few moments the evolutionary process. To observe the patience of the Divine Creator in working out the details of his plan may help us in comprehending more intelligently the methods of his providence, which accomplishes its vast results by the perfect supervision and control of every item that is related, however remotely, to the final issue.[1]

Let us review the creative process as if it were a picture or panorama passing before our mental vision. We will exclude all other worlds and systems from our sight, and fix our attention upon a single object in the vast realms of space. It looks like a little cloud, or a puff of smoke. Where the cosmic dust of which it is composed came from we do not know. It appears as if precipitated or con-

---

[1] I am aware that all authorities are not agreed in accepting the nebular hypothesis of creation. But there is no longer disagreement on one point, namely, that God's methods are not cataclysmal but gradual. Whatever may have been the method of creation, the process was unquestionably a manifestation of infinite power and infinite painstaking, and my sole purpose is to aid the reader in gaining a larger conception of the ways of a Supreme Being with whom "one day is as a thousand years, and a thousand years as one day."

densed from the interstellar ether like clouds from our terrestrial atmosphere. The most reasonable theory is that it was so evolved directly from the spiritual by the creative act of God. But we need not now concern ourselves about its origin. We are only watching to see what may be its history. As we look closely we observe that the mass has a rotary motion. The movement seems slow, but this is because of its immense distance from us. The "puff of smoke" is not less than three thousand million miles in diameter. How inconceivably distant must be our standpoint to reduce the mighty operation to a scale which our limited powers can appreciate! The time we are bridging is of the same vast measure as the space. It is not in the mind of man to conceive the cycles that have elapsed since the formation of our solar system was first begun.

The motion is in reality tremendous, and it eventually has the effect of causing a ring of the vapor to become separated from the main body. The law of attraction causes the ring to gradually gather itself together until it becomes a sphere, revolving on its axis, and moving in a circle around the central mass. In due course of time another ring is thrown off, which, in its turn, becomes a sphere moving in its orbit. Another and another ring is lost, the mass condensing each time, till at last it gathers within itself as a central globe, emitting a vast amount of heat and light.

Among the various revolving spheres our interest centers upon our own, the third from the sun. It, too, gathers and condenses, till it changes from a gaseous state to that of a globe of molten mineral. Our glance is a hasty one, and we can only notice how it gradually cools, shrinking as it cools, and thus forms the irregularities on the surface which we now know as mountains and valleys. From this point the past tense will be used in our description.

The condensation of the surrounding gases must have produced a strong glow of light. We thus have a scientific reason for the mention of light in the Scripture narrative before the sun is spoken of: "God said, Let there be light: and there was light. . . . And the evening and the morning were the first day."

The gases were gradually separated into two distinct substances—atmosphere and water. "God divided the waters which were under the firmament from the waters which were above the firmament: and it was so. And God called the firmament Heaven. And the evening and the morning were the second day. And God said, Let the waters under the heaven be gathered together unto one place, and let the dry land appear: and it was so. And God called the dry land Earth; and the gathering together of the waters called he Seas: and God saw that it was good."

By various processes which it is not necessary for our present purpose to describe, the surface of the solid portion of the globe was gradually disintegrated, and was thus made ready for a new application of the divine creative force.

And here we cannot but pause to lament the fatuity of those scientists who make such a strange use of their brilliant intellectual powers in striving to argue God out of existence, and to attribute all things to an inherent power in matter—a "gospel of dirt," as Carlyle fitly characterizes it. It may be instructive to turn aside for a moment and see how this subject is treated from the standpoint of the materialist. Mr. Grant Allen, in his "Life of Darwin," says:

"Here Biology steps in with its splendid explanation of organized life, as due essentially to the secondary action of radiated solar energy on the outer crust of such a cooling and evolving planet. Falling on the cells of the simplest green plants, the potent sunlight dissociates the carbon from the oxygen in the carbonic acid floating in the atmosphere, and builds it up with the hydrogen of water in the tissues of the organism into starches and other organic products, which differ from the inert substances around them mainly by the possession of locked-up solar energy. On the energy-yielding food-stuffs thus stored up the animal in turn feeds and battens, reducing what was before potential into actual motion, just as the steam-engine reduces the latent solar energy of coal into visible heat and visible movement in its furnace and its machinery. How the first organism came to exist Biology has not yet been able fully to explain for us; but, aided by chemical science, it has been able to show us in part how some of the simpler organic bodies may have been originally built up, and it does not despair of showing us in the end how the earliest organism may actually have been produced from the prime elements of oxygen, hydrogen, nitrogen, and carbon."

But, it may be asked, suppose Biology succeeds in showing how the earliest organism might have been thus produced, where are "the prime elements of oxygen, hydrogen, nitrogen, and carbon" supposed to come from? From the cosmic dust, of course. But who made the cosmic dust, and who caused its atoms to combine into these four "prime elements"? If the materialist turns upon us and says, "Suppose we acknowledge the maker to be God: will you tell us who made God?" our answer is at hand. We admit our incapacity to sound the infinite. But *we* have traced creation back to a rational starting-point, a sentient Being. To start with matter, making it self-creating and self-sustaining, is irrational and illogical. This we say without reference to a moral or spiritual kingdom, for which "the gospel of dirt" makes no provision and leaves no room.

It ought in justice to be stated that the passage quoted from Mr. Allen expresses his sentiments only, and not those of the great scientist whose biography he is writing. This he frankly admits, as follows: "Into this most fundamental of biological problems Darwin himself, with his constitutional caution and dread of speculative theorizing, was not careful or curious to enter." From other sources we learn that the great investigator had so completely surrendered his mind to the observation of facts and the consideration of external evidences that his spiritual faculties were apparently atrophied or paralyzed. He once said to his friend, the Duke of Argyll: "Sometimes I am overwhelmed with a sense of the presence of a personal God, and then" (with a sad shake of the head) "it seems to go away."

The time that elapsed before our globe was ready for the advent of life must have been inconceivable in its sum total. And when life appeared it was doubtless in accordance with God's invariable law "without observation." The simple forms which first came into being would hardly have been recognized as life had any one been there to witness. Yet they were the harbingers of the world's great springtime, foretelling the coming of all the future marvels of the vegetable and animal kingdoms. Slowly, one by one, the varying forms appeared and developed, till the glories of the plant world were fully manifested. "And God said, Let the earth bring forth grass, the herb yielding seed, and the fruit tree yielding fruit after his kind, whose seed is in itself, upon the earth: and it was so. . . . And the evening and the morning were the third day."

At this time the globe must have been surrounded by a dense cloud of glowing vapor. It was like a gigantic steam-bath. This was most favorable for the growth of vegetation, but was not a suitable condition for animal life. The vapor must roll together and partly disappear, leaving the sun free to shine through the clouds and cause portions of the earth to become dry and habitable. Could any description of this "clearing up" process equal that which we find in the Book of Genesis? "And God said, Let there be lights in the firmament of the heaven to divide the day from the night; and let them be for signs, and for seasons, and for days, and years: and let them be for lights in the firmament of the heaven to give light upon the earth: and it was so. And God made two great lights; the greater light to rule the day, and the lesser light to rule the night: he made the stars also. And God set them in the firmament of the heaven to give light upon the earth, and to rule over the day and over the night, and to divide the light from the darkness: and God saw that it was good. And the evening and the morning were the fourth day."

At last the period arrived for the advent of conscious life. The humblest and most primitive forms of animal life first appeared in the ocean, scarcely to be distinguished from the vegetable creation, and yet exhibiting the first stages of a development which was destined to continue reaching upward toward an ideal type till it was finally attained in the human form. "And God said, Let the waters bring forth abundantly the moving creature that hath life, and fowl that may fly above the earth in the open firmament of heaven. . . . And God made the beast of the earth after his kind, and cattle after their kind, and everything that creepeth upon the earth after his kind: and God saw that it was good."

And thus the culminating point was finally reached: "And God said, Let us make man in our image, after our likeness."

How was the divine spark first communicated? We cannot tell. We only know that "the first man Adam was made a living soul." The primitive race, fresh from the Creator's hand, appears to have been a simple people. They lived on the fruits of the field. They knew no wrong, and had open communication with their Divine Maker. But with their other endowments was included the power of choosing between good and evil, out of which godlike faculty grew the great drama of human life.

We have watched the puff of cosmic dust through its various changes, and have witnessed the evolution of our planet from a mass of mineral to a teeming world. The space covered by the solar system appears inconceivably great to our limited capacities. It is, in reality, a mere hand-breadth in the universe, as may be shown by a simple expedient. If we imagine the sun reduced to a pin's point and the orbits of the planets correspondingly contracted, the vast outreach of space can be made to appeal somewhat to the imagination. Starting with Mercury, and representing it as about two inches from the sun, the scale of distances will appear roughly as follows:

Mercury	2 inches.
Venus	3 "
Earth	4 "
Mars	6 "
Jupiter	21 "
Saturn	38 "
Uranus	79 "
Neptune	123 "
The nearest fixed star	*fourteen miles.*

No reduction of the perspective will enable us to form the slightest conception of this distance, which is but the beginning of our outlook. Yet, aside from the question of distances, we can form in our minds a general impression or picture of the material universe. We may imagine a vast space in which are innumerable groups of spheres, each group revolving around a brilliant sun, which in its turn is revolving with its family of planets around a greater sun. These groups are in all stages of creation, maturity, or decay. Some are still in the nebulous state. Some are partially developed. Some have passed the period of maturity and are in the process of extinction—dying stars. In this immensity our earth is, by comparison, a mere grain of sand on the seashore; a mote floating in a sunbeam. Can we microscopic creatures living upon its surface claim any share in a providential supervision which is occupied in momentarily creating and sustaining this boundless universe? Yes, we may; for in our essential being we do not belong to the material universe, but partake of the nature of Him who created it.

If any reader of these pages is troubled with doubts as to the validity of the theory of evolution, let him be reassured. Evolution with God as the creating and organizing force—that is, *Christian* evolution—is a doctrine that is widely and increasingly accepted by the best minds in all fields of thought, including the religious, as the only logical and consistent theory of creation. The Rev. Dr. McCosh, late president of Princeton College, in a recent work entitled "The Religious Aspect of Evolution," says:

When I was called from the Old World to the presidency of an important college in America, I had to consider—I remember seriously pondering the perplexity in the vessel which brought me to this country—whether I should at once avow my convictions, or keep them in abeyance because of the prejudices of religious men, and lest I might unsettle the faith of the students committed to my care. I decided to pursue the open and honest course, being sure that it would be best in the end. I was not a week in Princeton till I let it be known to the upper classes of the college that I was in favor of evolution properly limited and explained, and I have proclaimed my views in lectures and papers in a number of cities and before various associations, literary and religious. I have been gratified to find that none of the churches has assailed me, and this has convinced me that their doubts about evolution have proceeded mainly from the bad use to which the doctrine has been turned. I am pleased to discover that intelligent Christians are coming round gradually to the views which I have had the courage to publish.

I have all along had a sensitive apprehension that the undiscriminating denunciation from so many pulpits, periodicals, and seminaries might drive some of our thoughtful young men to infidelity, as they clearly saw development everywhere in nature, and were at the same time told by their advisers that they could not believe in evolution and yet be Christians. I am gratified beyond measure to find that I am thanked by my pupils, some of whom have reached the highest position as naturalists, because in showing them evolution in the works of God, I showed them that this was not inconsistent with religion, and thus enabled them to follow science and yet retain their faith in the Bible.

Evolution is in accordance with all of nature's methods and analogies. It also has its counterpart in the mental and spiritual development of mankind. It even affords a new argument for the immortality of the soul. This argument is presented with striking force by Professor John

Fiske in his treatise on " The Destiny of Man." His views may be briefly summarized as follows:

Evolution shows a continuous process of development in physical life from the simplest forms through a constantly ascending series till a consummation is attained in the human structure. From that point the development changes from body growth to soul growth. In this direction there is no conceivable limit. ' " Has all the vast work that has led up to man gone for nothing? Is it a bubble that bursts, a vision that fades? To deny the everlasting persistence of the spiritual element in man is to rob the whole process of evolution of its meaning. To believe in the immortality of the soul is a supreme act of faith in the reasonableness of God's work."

The Rev. Francis G. Peabody, D.D., in a discourse on the text " The earnest expectation of the creation waiteth for the revealing of the sons of God," says:

This verse might be described as St. Paul's statement of the doctrine of evolution. Of course it would be quite absurd to claim for the Apostle any clear expression of the modern doctrine. No doubt the universe presents a very different picture to us from any which his mind could see, and it would be foolish to force his words into our modern ways of thought. Of course, moreover, he is in this passage primarily thinking only of his little church at Rome, and giving them rules for their duty and loyalty, or what he calls "the law of the spirit of life in Christ Jesus." And yet, with the mind of a great philosopher, or rather with the vision of a great prophet, he is swept beyond the special case before him into the general principle which it involves, and in giving rules to Rome he is led to survey the method of the universe. The whole creation, he says, groans and travails in pain until now, as though it bore within itself the burden of the life that was to follow. It is to him what he calls an expectant creation—a prophetic, anticipatory world. In the inanimate world there is, he thinks, a kind of dumb sympathy with the sin and struggle and redemption of man. Its history and process point on to the experience of man. Thus, in a large, poetic way, the universe looks to him like a connected and a growing whole, the life of man finding its prophecy and likeness in the life of things, and the life of the lower creation reaching up at last into the experience of man, and thus, it may be fairly said, there is at least a curious foreshadowing of ways of thought which have now grown familiar. Two things, however, seem to mark the Apostle's doctrine. First, this whole creation of which he writes is to him not a dead, but a living, thing. Its movement is not the movement of machinery, but the movement of life. It groans and travails with its desire to fulfil itself. It is, he says, earnestly expectant; it waits for that which is to come. It is a sympathetic, a patient world. Instead of a blind, purposeless, mechanical process, this man sees a universe with an intention and desire of its own, bringing forth at last, through the pains which we now call the struggle for existence, the state of things we see. Instead of a world-factory grinding out with indifference its tides and storms, its plants and animals, and the emotions and ideals of men, he sees a Universe working out with expectancy and desire a divinely appointed end. Thus he simply anticipates the whole series of philosophers and poets who have seen in nature a living and purposeful process, manifesting at each step the presence of one comprehensive will. It might have been St. Paul instead of Herbert Spencer who wrote of "the naturally revealed end toward which the power manifested in evolution works." It might have been St. Paul instead of Tennyson who sang of

> One far-off divine event
> Toward which the whole creation moves.

The second mark of the Pauline doctrine is still more interesting. How is this purpose of creation, the Apostle seems to ask himself, to be completed? Having reached its present point, for what does it now wait? The expectant creation, he answers, waits for the revealing of the sons of God. And who are the sons of God? He has just told us that in another verse: "As many as are led by the Spirit of God, they are the sons of God." The sons of God, then, are simply the people led by God's Spirit—people lifted by God, that is to say, into the higher capacities of their own spiritual life; and for such people, he announces, the whole creation waits. Without them the universal evolution pauses in its course. So runs his extraordinary statement of the method of creation.

When we have once gained a clear conception of all that is involved in the theory of the divine immanence, we can never again be satisfied with the old mechanical view, but are ready to exclaim with Goethe:

No! such a God my worship may not win
Who lets the world about his finger spin,
A thing extern; my God must rule within;
And whom I own for Father, God, Creator,
Hold nature in himself, himself in nature;
And, in his kindly arms embraced, the whole
Doth live and move by his pervading soul.

CHAPTER III.

WHY THE SCHOOL-HOUSE WAS BUILT.

WHY was this educational institution founded and established? For what purpose was the stupendous work of creation conceived and executed?

A literal interpretation of the Book of Genesis gives the impression that God tried an experiment and failed. But the revelations of science show that a literal rendering is impossible. Should this be permitted to weaken our faith in the Bible as an inspired book? On the contrary, it is one of the strongest proofs of the divine origin of the book. If it had been written by a man or by any number of men without divine illumination, the language would necessarily have conformed to the state of knowledge at the period of their writing, whenever that happened to be. Observe, in contrast with that method, the supreme wisdom of the Divine Author of the book in the account of creation. An outline picture is given in simple yet poetic language, appealing at once to the religious sentiment of the reader and to the sense of the sublime which so strongly characterized the Oriental mind, and yet accurate in its suggestions; a sketch to be filled out in succeeding ages, as the hidden mysteries and unknown laws of the universe were gradually revealed.

If the opposite plan had been followed and the facts had been stated literally, or as they actually occurred, what would have been the result? The divine revelation would have been rejected. The human race was totally unprepared for the reception of astronomical truth. To ask the ancients to believe that the world was a sphere floating in space would have appeared to them an insult to their intelligence.

The instinct of conservatism is one of God's gifts to the human race, to balance the love of novelty and to avert the dangers that arise from the attractiveness of new theories and new experiences. But, like all of God's gifts, it should be wisely used. It is one thing to defend the Bible and quite another to defend all the past interpretations of it. There was a time when belief in witchcraft was universal. Certain portions of the Bible, written during that period, conformed in its phraseology to this belief. Increased intelligence among the people showed the folly of such a superstition. Must the old interpretations be retained after the occasion for them has passed away? John Wesley insisted that the Bible must stand or fall with witchcraft, as it taught that if it taught anything. Witchcraft has disappeared, but the Bible remains, unshorn of its strength.

When geology began to show that, instead of six days, the world must have been many millions of years in the process of formation, devout men on all sides sprang forward to defend the Bible. So they supposed, but they were only defending an interpretation of its words which suited the "times of men's ignorance," but which must inevitably give way as knowledge increased. One zealous "defender" went so far as to claim that God placed fossil specimens among the rocks to test our faith and to show whether we would stand by the truth even against the evidence of our senses.

It is well to remember that our ideas concerning the primal history of the race are rather Miltonic than scriptural. Out of the wealth of his boundless imagination Milton wove a splendid romance of which but a small portion has any warrant in the statements of the Scriptures. Yet the creations of his genius have fastened themselves upon our minds as veritable truths, and the theory which underlies his story gives a strong coloring to all our ideas on the subject. As the best means of freeing our thoughts from this influence let us lay aside for the moment all previous impressions and consider the case hypothetically, conceiving a plan or theory which appears consistent with God's character as revealed in his Word and in his dealings with mankind.

As a Being of infinite wisdom, goodness, and love, he could not be imagined as existing without the exercise of those qualities or attributes. For this purpose there must be sentient beings toward whom such qualities could be directed. But in order to have them he must create them, for he is the only self-existent Being. What order of creatures would serve this purpose? Evidently, they must have intelligence and a capacity to receive and reciprocate his love. In other words, they must have qualities similar to his own; they must be made in his image. But mere characterless reflections of the divine qualities would not be sufficient. Some means must be devised by which the reflected character could be so changed as to become personal and individual. How could this be accomplished? By so excluding these created beings from the consciousness of their relation to God and to the spiritual world that they would be compelled to exercise a personal responsibility. They must be left at liberty to choose between good and evil. Having learned through a process of discipline to choose good for its own sake, they would no longer be like infinitesimal mirrors, reflecting a character not their own, but would become independent beings, with a dignity based upon their essential personality, worthy of the divine companionship, and fitted to work with their Creator in carrying out his beneficent plans and purposes.

Can this description be regarded as merely hypothetical? Is it not rather an inevitable conclusion from a careful study of the Bible and of our own nature?

Dr. Lyman Abbott says: "We do not believe in a God who has been trying experiments and failed. We believe that God made the world. We believe that he created the human race. We believe that he is a God of foresight and wisdom. We believe that he knew what he was about when he made the world; that he knew what he was about when he made the human race; and that he made the world and made the human race because the product of that making was going to be a larger life, a nobler life, and therefore a more blessed and a more happy life; that in the very beginning, when he sowed the seeds, he knew what kind of harvest was going to grow out of it, and he was not one that sowed the seeds of tares, but one who knew that the wheat would overbalance the tares in the last great harvest."

Such a plan appeals to our highest reason and serves as a key to many of the most obscure and difficult passages in the sacred Scriptures. It also throws a flood of light upon the laws and methods of Divine Providence. We see why it is that while we *seem* to be shut away from God's direct care, it is impossible that we are so in reality. Science shows how we are sustained in our physical being every instant by the Supreme Power which first created us. If this should be suddenly removed, our bodies would disappear. They would not return to dust; they would return to nothing. The smallest particle of dust exists only by virtue of the divine power which created it and holds it together by the act of God which we call attraction.

Under the theory of the divine immanence, the declarations of the Bible concerning God's supervision of human events are not arbitrary, but scientific. There could be no human beings and therefore no human events but, for the perpetual exercise of his creating and sustaining power. In the light of this truth how sublime and uplifting are such words as these:

"Underneath thee are the everlasting arms." (Deut. xxxiii. 27.)

"A man's heart deviseth his way, but the Lord directeth his steps." (Prov. xvi. 9.)

"Man's goings are of the Lord; how can a man then understand his own way?" (Prov. xx. 24.)

"O Lord, I know that the way of man is not in himself: it is not in man that walketh to direct his steps." (Jer. x. 23.)

"Except the Lord build the house, they labor in vain that build it: except the Lord keep the city, the watchman waketh but in vain." (Ps. cxxvii. 1.)

We can, it is true, deprive ourselves of all comfort in such declarations by a simple process. We can refuse to believe them because our finite powers are unable to comprehend how they are to be reconciled with man's freedom. Such skepticism was natural and almost inevitable before the law of evolution was discovered and applied.

A gigantic Deity somewhere in space, who, although described as infinite, was yet regarded as separate from the objects of his creation, and working by arbitrary laws and rules—such a conception of God left room for innumerable doubts and difficulties. Science, by revealing the methods of an immanent God, has destroyed the middle ground of shadowy doubts, and has made a clear and distinct issue between perfect faith and absolute disbelief. He who believes in God must believe that he is in all things, for science shows that the Unseen Power is and must be universal. The Christian believes the Unseen Power to be a divine Father; a Being of perfect wisdom and love. Then he must accept the testimony of science, which confirms to the utmost limit of their meaning every word of the Bible which says or implies that God controls every atom in the universe and directs the smallest circumstance of every human life. How this truth is to be reconciled with the other truth of which every one is conscious, that we are also free to act, and responsible for our actions, it is not for us to know. Truly, it is a mystery, but it is no more a mystery than life itself. We accept life in spite of the fact that we do not understand it. So must we accept the universality of Divine Providence, and build our lives upon that foundation if we wish to be either consistent or contented. The fatal flaw in our judgment of Divine Providence arises from our tendency to narrow our view of it down to the temporary experiences of earthly life. We are like children trying to judge their parents' action from the standpoint of the nursery or the school-room. The case is a very simple one if we will but consider it in the light of the truth and of our own professed faith. In order to prepare us for an eternal companionship with the divine, and to train our faculties and powers for usefulness in the heavenly world, God has, with infinite wisdom, constructed a material universe in which we are to remain for a little time and learn the lessons of love, obedience, and self-denial which are essential to our eternal happiness. But instead of accepting life on this basis, what do we do? We straightway begin to make this brief and evanescent period the center of all our plans, hopes, and expectations. The habit is so strong that even after we profess to surrender earthly hopes and to devote ourselves to the interests of eternity, we are still constantly tempted to estimate God's providential dealings from the standpoint of this "cooling cinder" which we call our home.

The official report of a benevolent association in New York describes the following case:

> A cultivated woman had supported herself during forty years of widowhood by teaching in Western cities. She had come East to pass her declining years with a relative. We found her alone in a noisy tenement, in feeble health, without fire in midwinter, subsisting on bread and water for weeks together. "I have suffered so much from cold and privation since my sight began to fail," she said, "that I found myself doubting whether there be a God at all. Now, to have a room, rent free, with fire and food, seems like a beautiful dream!" And the tears coursed down her thin cheeks as she added: "I feel now ashamed to have doubted his existence!"

This would doubtless be quoted as an evidence of God's providential care. He permitted her to suffer in order to develop her faith and patience, and then, in the last extremity, brought relief. But suppose no relief had come, and she had died of cold and hunger, as many do: would this have indicated any less love on the part of her Heavenly Father? Would it have given reason to believe that God had deserted her? Assuredly not. If it was right to test her faith and patience thus far, it would have been no evidence of indifference or neglect if the discipline had been carried still farther. Would it have been any less indicative of divine care if she had been taken to the heavenly mansions instead of being left in this world, even with the luxury of " a room rent free, with fire and food "? Yet if she had been found dead of starvation, the event would have been spoken of as a " mysterious providence " even by many Christian people, whose faith should supply a key to all such problems.

At the time of the terrible disaster of the Conemaugh flood universal comment was excited by the touching case of a little girl whose mother was about setting her adrift on the raging waters as the only chance of saving her. " Will God take care of me?" said the frightened child. " Yes, darling, he will," was the heart-stricken mother's reply. What better care could he possibly take than to remove her from *all* earthly disasters and place her among the shining ones in the heavenly kingdom? Yet as the child was not saved, the world could see no " Providence " in it. If it had been caught in a side current and finally rescued, the event would have been heralded far and wide as one of the " remarkable providences." It would have been quoted as a striking evidence of God's providential care, thus giving the totally erroneous impression that his care was exercised toward those who were saved, while the others were left to the inexorable laws of nature.

The circumstances and events of this life can never be correctly measured from the earthly standpoint. Our thoughts must be transferred in imagination beyond the veil of the spiritual in order to secure a point of view from which to see the things of this world in their true relations.

Let the reader thus place himself in thought beyond the material barrier which separates us from the world of spiritual realities. Standing there, with the infinite ages of eternity before us, we can look back and see that the years of this life are " as a tale that is told," and all its occurrences, which seem to us so important at the moment, are insignificant in comparison with the unending experiences of the life to come. Whether we reach that world through the pains of a lingering disease, by a startling casualty in which others are destroyed with us, or through the natural decay of old age—the special method of our removal is a matter of small concern as compared with the infinite realities which await us on the other side.

The first thing to be done in a study of the laws of Divine Providence is to rid ourselves entirely of the misleading impression that God's original plans for this world were in any way thwarted or interfered with. No rational view of the subject can be obtained on that basis. The material universe was developed through a slow history of untold ages by the power of God working within it. The spiritual life of the human race is passing through the same process of growth under the control of the same laws. The providence of an infinite God includes every atom of the material world, and every individual of the race. If it is scientific to study the ways of God in nature, it is no less scientific to study the ways of God in humanity. As a guide or help in such study it is necessary to keep in mind certain truths, laws, or principles, which may be stated in the following propositions:

1. God is infinite and omnipresent. All things exist from him.

2. God is love, and all his purposes and plans are the

expressions of that quality united with and guided by infinite wisdom.

3. His plans embrace eternity, and cannot therefore be measured or judged by the standards of time.

4. His purposes with regard to the human family have reference to their eternal life. Their experiences in this world are used solely for spiritual ends with a view to preparing them for the permanent life of the world to come.

5. Man's highest destiny, as a being made in the image of God, can only be attained by allowing him perfect liberty of choice and action. This leaves him free to follow evil, and thus permits him to bring unhappiness to himself and to all who are associated with him, including the animal creation.

6. God's promise to the human race is that he will superintend the life of every individual, either leading him to the highest good which he in the exercise of his choice will permit, or, if he persists in choosing evil, his evil will be restrained, limited, and overruled.

Herbert Spencer says: "The existence of an eternal Power back of all phenomena is the one certain element of our knowledge." It is the privilege of the Christian to recognize in this eternal Power of the scientist the Heavenly Father of the Scriptures, and it is his pleasing duty in this grand age of increasing knowledge to study his Father's ways from the standpoint of science as well as of experience.

CHAPTER IV.

A HUMAN GOD AND A HUMANE FATHER—A REASONABLE ANTHROPOMORPHISM.

TWO fears were excited in the minds of Christian people by the theory of evolution when it was first promulgated: it appeared to either banish God from the universe—a triumph of materialism—or to rob him of all personal qualities by proving him to be only a diffused influence—a triumph of pantheism.

Both fears were groundless. Instead of banishing the Creator from the universe, evolution gives a thousand arguments for his presence there, by showing his methods in creating and sustaining the myriad worlds and their infinitely varied contents. Belief in the personality of God is not lessened by recognizing his direct action in all the operations of nature any more than belief in the existence of the sun is diminished by a knowledge of the chemical laws by which its light and heat are transformed into vegetable life. As between Christians who accept the theory of evolution and those who do not, the belief of the former in a divine personality is no less clear and emphatic than is the faith of the latter. But neither the one class nor the other can undertake to define it. As God is infinite, his personality must be an infinite personality, and who can bring that within the limits of mortal imagination? Yet we still insist that he is *human*. In the works of creation we see evidences of consciousness, of will, of purpose—qualities which are reflected in the depths of our own being. Man can make a machine which will act as his obedient servant. It will weave a piece of cloth or propel a ship. But the Divine Creator calls into being an insect and endows it with more than a human prevision and with more than a mathematician's judgment and skill. It gathers its harvest in due season, and makes a cell for storing it in which the highest laws of geometry are anticipated and applied. Our steam-engine wears out, and must be replaced by another. God's honey-gatherer is a self-perpetuating creation. It has the power to reproduce itself to the end of time. Why pursue the illustration? What God has done in the universe is evidently the work of one whose qualities are similar to our own, but on an infinite scale; in other words, they give us an impression of a human God.

Is this human God also humane? Look at the universality of suffering. "Nothing can be clearer than that nature is full of cruelty and maladaptation. In every part of the animal world we find implements of torture surpassing in devilish ingenuity anything that was ever seen in the dungeons of the Inquisition. We are introduced to a scene of incessant and universal strife of which it is not apparent on the surface that the outcome is the good or the happiness of anything that is sentient."[1]

A single phrase in the foregoing description affords a clue to the difficult problem—*on the surface*. We are as nothing when compared with the infinite, and the narrow scope of our vision gives us no hint of the outreach of an infinite plan. When we see so many evidences of a loving

[1] John Fiske.

prevision and supervision in "the works of creation and providence," it is not difficult to believe that a humane God should permit evil and suffering as part of a great design for some beneficent end. The scoffer will scoff, whatever happens. A noted infidel, on being asked what improvement he thought he could have made in the world if he had created it, replied, "I would have made health catching instead of disease." This is precisely what our Divine Creator has done, except that he has applied the law to our spiritual nature instead of the physical. He created the universe for the development of our souls, while the materialist would have made it merely the servant of our bodies. There is not a growing human being who has not "caught" a large share of his spiritual health from other and nobler souls. Emerson says: "There needs but one wise man in a company, and all are wise, so rapid is the contagion." Even the sickness of the body is often a means of ministering to the health of the soul. What miraculous patience, heroic trust, and heavenly tenderness do we often see as a result of bodily sufferings, grievous and long continued.

Mr. S. Laing of Edinburgh writes as follows concerning the anthropomorphic idea in his work on "Modern Science and Modern Thought":

> Not only has faith been shaken in the supernatural as a direct and immediate agent in the phenomena of the worlds of matter and of life, but the demonstration of the "struggle for life" and "survival of the fittest" has raised anew, and with vastly augmented force, those questions as to the moral constitution of the universe and the origin of evil which have so long exercised the highest minds. Is it true that "love" is "creation's final law," when we find this enormous and apparently prodigal waste of life going on; these cruel internecine battles between individuals and species in the struggle for existence; this cynical indifference of nature to suffering? There are, approximately, thirty-six hundred millions of deaths of human beings

in every century, of whom at least twenty percent., or seven hundred and twenty millions die before they have attained to clear self-consciousness and conscience. What becomes of them? Why were they born? Are they nature's failures, and "cast as rubbish to the heap"?

To such questions there is no answer. We are obliged to admit that as the material universe is not, as we once fancied, measured by our standards and regulated at every turn by an intelligence resembling ours, so neither is the moral universe to be explained by simply magnifying our own moral ideas, and explaining everything by the action of a Being who does what we should have done in his place. If we insist on this anthropomorphic conception we are driven to this dilemma. Carlyle bases his belief in a God, "the infinite Good One," on this argument: "All that is good, generous, wise, right—whatever I deliberately and forever love in others and myself, who or what could by any possibility have given it to me but One who first had it to give? This is not logic. This is axiom."

But how of the evil? No sincere man, looking into the depths of his own soul, or at the facts of the world around, can doubt that along with much that is good, generous, wise, and right there is much that is bad, base, foolish, and wrong. If logic compels us to receive as axiom a good author for the former, does not the same logic equally compel us to accept the axiom that the author of the latter must have been one who "first had it himself to give"? That is, we must accept the theory of a God who is half good, half evil, or adopt the Zoroastrian conception of a universe contested by an Ormuzd and Ahriman, a good and evil principle, whose power is, for the present at any rate, equally balanced.

From this dilemma there is no escape, unless we give up altogether the idea of an anthropomorphic deity, and adopt frankly the scientific idea of a First Cause, inscrutable and past finding out, and of a universe whose laws we can trace, but of whose real essence we know nothing, and can only suspect or faintly discern a fundamental law which may make the polarity of good and evil a necessary condition of existence.

The weakness of this argument is its own sufficient refutation. The question cannot be settled by writing deity with a small "d" and transferring the dignity of capitals to a diffused and therefore inconceivable First Cause. It is a new discovery of Mr. Laing that axiom is based upon logic. One of the grandest results of the evolution of modern thought is the release of psychology from the swaddling-bands of metaphysics, "the sinuosities of scholastic logic." The soul is now treated as an entity, and not as an abstraction. Its powers are as real and as little subject to the scalpel of the metaphysical hair-splitter as gravitation or electricity. As surely as the eye has a capacity for seeing light just so surely has the soul a capacity for seeing God. This truth has been recognized by a few choice spirits in all ages. The difference between the past and the present is in the wider diffusion of this gift of sight. What Plato saw, what Carlyle saw, is now becoming an open vision to the race. Men see God because they are made in his image and have a capacity for receiving an impression of him as the optic nerve is adapted to receive an impression of light. Mr. Laing's deduction of an evil God is gratuitous and needless. It is neither logical nor axiomatic. A responsible being with the power of choice—a capability of choosing God—creates evil the moment he rejects him and follows his own selfish way. The materialists deny immortality and then accuse God of injustice because he fails to solve the problems of life within the time they assign for it. The Christian introduces the factor of eternity, and comprehends that the sum total of suffering in this world, vast as it seems, may be no more than the prick of a pin in comparison with the inconceivably greater sum of good which is to follow.

We may accept it as an established truth that the God of science, equally with the God of the Bible, is a human God and a humane Father. We cannot measure him, because he is infinite; but we can understand him in all that concerns our responsibility and happiness. There is a rational anthropomorphism which satisfies all requirements.

Against the hopeless words of the author just quoted let us read the profound analysis of Professor Fiske:

"It is enough to remind the reader that Deity is unknowable just in so far as it is not manifested to consciousness through the phenomenal world—knowable just in so far as it is thus manifested; unknowable in so far as infinite and absolute—knowable in the order of its phenomenal manifestations; knowable, in a symbolic way, as the Power which is disclosed in every throb of the mighty rhythmic life of the universe; knowable as the eternal Source of a moral law which is implicated with each action of our lives, and in obedience to which lies our only guaranty of the happiness which is incorruptible, and which neither inevitable misfortune nor unmerited obloquy can take away. Thus, though we may not by searching find out God, though we may not compass infinitude or attain to absolute knowledge, we may at least know all that it concerns us to know as intelligent and responsible beings. They who seek to know more than this, to transcend the conditions under which alone is knowledge possible, are, in Goethe's profound language, as wise as little children, who, when they have looked into a mirror, turn it around to see what is behind it."

CHAPTER V.

WHERE IS GOD?

It is not easy to gain an intelligent and satisfying conception of God's relation to us. Our thoughts are so adjusted to the limitations of time and space that when we read of the "Most High God," "the hills from whence cometh our help," and many similar expressions in the Bible, we involuntarily think of a spatial elevation rather than of that which is moral or spiritual. So far as we are influenced by that standard, the stronger the impression we have of God's greatness and majesty the farther away from us will he appear to be removed. It is scarcely possible to have true ideas on the subject of Divine Providence unless this impression of distance is eradicated. The question, Where is God? should therefore be considered before entering upon a study of his providential methods in the world.

Great as are the difficulties which surround this subject, they are not insurmountable. There are certain lines of thought and illustrations from nature which embody or suggest principles from which a true idea of God's relation to us and to the universe can be derived.

The first illustration is man himself. "God created man in his own image." If this is true, it must be that a proper study of ourselves will teach us many things about God. As a help in solving the problem of God's relation to the universe, let us consider carefully the relation of the soul to the body.

The first thing to be done is to reverse our former ideas on the subject by considering the question, Are we bodies, or are we spirits? We were formerly supposed to be bodies inhabited by spirits. The newer and truer teaching is that we are spirits purely, the body being only a temporary adaptation to a material environment.

> We are spirits clad in veils;
> Man by man was never seen;
> All our deep communing fails
> To remove the shadowy screen.

Professor John Fiske, speaking from the standpoint of the scientist, says:

"That the soul cannot be the product of any cunning arrangement of material particles is demonstrated beyond peradventure by what we now know of the correlation of physical forces. The teaching of Plato that the soul is a spiritual substance, an effluence from the divine which under certain circumstances becomes incarnated in perishable forms of matter, is doubtless the view most consonant with the present state of our knowledge."

Plato's own language is this: "God made the soul in origin and existence prior to the body, to be the ruler and the mistress, of whom the body was to be the subject."

The body is no more the man than the sea-diver's dress is the diver. The dress is a necessary adaptation to the element in which he is to do his work. Its glass eyes admit the light; its hands move about and accomplish the purpose for which the descent into the sea is made. But the diver within is the soul, the spirit, the man. It is his eye that sees and his hand that moves. If we afterward see the dress lying on the shore, we feel no interest in it except as a temporary expedient for achieving a certain result. Just so it is with our body: it is our earthly dress —only that and nothing more. How beautifully is this truth expressed by the Persian poet:

> Faithful friends, it lies, I know,
> Pale and white, and cold as snow;
> And ye say, "Abdallah's dead,"—
> Weeping at the feet and head.
> I can see your falling tears;
> I can hear your sighs and prayers;
> Yet I smile and whisper this:
> "I am not the thing you kiss!
> Cease your tears and let it lie;
> It was *mine*,—it is not *I*."
>
> Sweet friends, what the women lave
> For the last sleep of the grave
> Is a hut which I am quitting,
> Is a garment no more fitting,
> Is a cage from which at last,
> Like a bird, my soul has passed.
> Love the inmate, not the room;
> The wearer, not the garb; the plume
> Of the eagle, not the bars
> That keep him from the splendid stars.
>
> Loving friends, oh, rise and dry
> Straightway every weeping eye;
> What ye lift upon the bier
> Is not worth one single tear.
> 'Tis an empty sea-shell,—one
> Out of which the pearl is gone.
> The shell is broken, it lies there;
> The pearl, the *all*, the *soul*, is *here*.

The soul is the life of the body. It must therefore be in every part of the body. It does the entire work of building up and sustaining the bodily structure. It is in all the organs, performing their various functions. It is in the arteries, transporting the blood to every part of the system. It is the cunning workman that carries every particle of nutritive matter to exactly the right place, and employs it to construct a bone, a muscle, a nerve, whatever is needed in that particular spot. Even the outer skin, which has no feeling in itself, and seems hardly to have any life, is constructed by the soul as a wonderful wall to protect the delicate tissues of the body from exposure to cold and heat.

Perhaps the reader is saying to himself: " It seems strange to think of my soul as in my hand, my foot, and all parts of my body. I thought my soul was my *mind*, which does the thinking. My hand and foot cannot think. I have imagined my soul as in the brain, creating thoughts, and in the heart, inspiring sweet affections." This is true, and it is just the truth that will help us presently to answer our question, Where is God? The soul acts throughout the body, but its *home* is where we think and feel. We often say of a person who has an animated expression, " His soul is in his face." It looks out of the eyes. It expresses itself by a smile. But its expression is by no means confined to the face. Are not our gestures often stronger than words? Do not our feet carry us on errands of mercy to those who need our help? Are not our hands obedient and faithful servants to minister in a thousand ways to those we love?

Here, then, we have the answer to our question, Where is God? *God's Spirit is in the universe as our soul is in our body.* Every part and particle of the universe was created by him and does his will just as our bodies were formed by our souls and obey our wills. The law called cohesive attraction is God's way of bringing particles of matter together to form earth, stone, wood, or any other substance. It is God's life in the seed which causes it to germinate and to give out tiny leaves which grow and unfold day and night till a plant, a flower, a tree, is produced. It is just as much God's love which creates a beautiful rose as it is our love which leads us to carry the rose to a sick friend.

And as in small things so in the larger. The principle called gravitation is God holding the planets in their places. All the mighty forces of the universe are only different ways in which God works, just as every motion of our body is caused by the soul within. Heat, light, color, sound, electricity, are various methods by which God manifests himself and accomplishes his purposes in the universe. We must not think a stroke of lightning is any less a direct act of God because we happen to know that it is electricity. Electricity is one of his many servants. "Fire and hail, snow and vapor, stormy wind fulfilling his word."

But this truth or theory excites in us somewhat the same feeling that we had with regard to ourselves. We did not like to think of a soul diffused through our bodies, and we do not like to think of a God diffused through the universe. The difficulty is imaginary. It does not exist in the latter case any more than in the former. Although the soul acts in every part of the body, its home is where it thinks and feels. It is so with our Heavenly Father. He acts in every part of the universe, but his home is where he thinks and feels. Does this seem hard to understand? We do not need to understand it. It is just as hard to understand the relation of the soul to the body as to understand the relation of God to the universe. Yet we do not doubt having a soul, for we are conscious that it thinks and feels. So we cannot reasonably doubt the existence of a Being in the universe who thinks and feels. We see innumerable evidences of his controlling and directing power and influence.

Our ideas concerning him may be still further helped by another illustration.

God is sometimes spoken of in the Bible as a sun. Let us follow the line of thought which is suggested by this comparison.

The sun is God's instrument for creating every particle of vegetable and animal life that exists on the earth. Not the smallest bit of moss or fern growing in some deep ravine, so shielded by rocks and trees that it never even saw the sun, but owes its birth and being entirely to the light and heat of that wonderful orb. By these subtle forces the particles of soil are drawn up from the earth and used to form the plant, tree, or flower. By their marvelous and mysterious chemistry the elements of matter are so combined as to produce the myriad forms of grace, beauty, and usefulness which are to be seen in the world. Every twig, bush, vine, tree, the flowers with their exquisite colors and fragrance, all the fruits of the earth, from the strawberry to the cocoanut, every insect and animal up to man himself—in a word, every particle of life on all this round globe is produced and sustained by the sun. It may therefore be truly said that the sun is *in* every form of life in the world. Yet the sun is a distinct body in the heavens, and thus we see why it is such a beautiful and suggestive symbol and representative of God. His *power* working in the universe is symbolized by the sun's light and heat, his *personality* by the orb from which they emanate. God's wisdom and love are the light and warmth by which our lives are blessed and our souls are made to grow. The sunlight penetrates everywhere. We do not have to send up petitions to the sun asking for light. It is poured down upon the earth in floods. We have only to open our shutters and it comes into our homes with all its beneficent influence. Just so does our Heavenly Father shed his love upon the evil and the good. The Bible declares that he *is* love. The sun is fire, and cannot help shining. God is love, and cannot help loving. The object of the sun is to send light and heat upon the earth and make things grow. So God's purpose is to send his love into our hearts and make us grow. But *we must open the shutters.* " Unto you that *fear my name* shall the Sun of righteousness arise with healing in his wings." The word "fear" does not in this case mean anything of the nature of dread or terror. It means the feeling which leads us to obey God, and we cannot obey him without loving him. If we desire, ever so feebly and imperfectly, to do his will, then we may think of him as our sun, sending his love every moment, trying to make us grow in everything that is good and beautiful. We will pray to him, for that is natural, but we do not need to beg for blessings as if he were unwilling to grant them. We should rather pray that he will open our hearts that we may take in the good gifts he is so anxious to bestow. They who hunger and thirst after righteousness are sure to be filled.

The remarkable suitability of the sun as a symbol of the Supreme Being becomes more apparent the more closely it is scrutinized. The beautiful and beneficent sunlight is turned by some plants into poison. So may we pervert God's beautiful gifts into evil and hurtful things. It is profitable to dwell much upon this conception of God. It leads to a true and clear idea of the methods of Divine Providence. It rids our minds of the medieval picture of an arbitrary ruler. The sun (we may say) desires to be only a blessing to the world. Its rays are charged with life, health, and beauty. But the degree of blessing depends wholly upon the way in which the light is received and used. It may be used to create a lovely flower or a noxious weed. Clay is hardened by the sun's heat, while wax is softened by it. The passages of Scripture which *seem* to indicate an arbitrary use of power by our Heavenly Father only express a universal law. The trials and afflictions of Moses were received with humility, and therefore they ennobled him. The trials and afflictions of Pharaoh were received with pride and stubbornness, and his heart was hardened.

Let us consider a little more fully the relation of the soul to the body. If one should be asked the question, "Where is your soul?" and the answer should be returned, "In my body," the reply would at first thought be regarded as correct. Yet in reality it is far from correct. The soul is not, and cannot, be confined within this body, nor even limited to the earth. Why? Because the soul is of an essentially different nature from the body. The body is limited to time and space, but the soul is not. The body belongs to this world. It is made of earth, and after the soul is done using it the earth will claim it again. The soul in its nature or essence has nothing in common with the body. It belongs to a totally different world, the *world of thoughts and affections.* It is indicative of the low stage of spiritual development attained by the human race that this inner world is commonly regarded as an unreal and shadowy world. On the contrary, it is the only real and substantial world. It is the only world that lasts. The "eternal hills" are made of crumbling dust, but the world of thoughts and affections will abide forever. The body-world is a very restricted world, but the soul-world is practically unlimited. It takes several weeks to carry the body to China, but if we have a friend in that country, our loving thought can go there in an instant. Our bodies are limited to a very small space on this small planet, but our thought can reach out to the farthest star.

The truth is (and it is a most important truth to realize), our souls belong as much to the spiritual world now as they ever will. They are confined within a body, it is true, but it is only temporarily, and for certain definite purposes. When these purposes are accomplished the body will drop off, and the soul will be freed from its earthly limitations. It will not go to any other material abode. There is no distant star or great central location among the circling orbs of heaven to which it will take its flight, as imaginative writers sometimes suggest. If that were the case, it would still be limited to this material universe. But it will *be* somewhere. Its environment of cosmic dust will disappear, and it will stand forth in the world of realities to which it belongs.

The Rev. Oliver Dyer has expressed this truth very clearly and forcibly as follows: "We naturally look upon material substances as the only substances, and whatever we cannot grasp with our senses we instinctively think to be unsubstantial; whereas the actual truth of the matter is that the spiritual is the only substantial, the only enduring, substance. Substantial means that which stands under, or *substands*. It means that which is the support of something else which needs to be supported. Our spirit is that which substands or supports our body and gives it its life—gives it all the life it has. As soon as the spirit, which is the *substand* of the body, is taken away, the body can no longer stand, because it has no standing-power of its own; and so the body then falls and goes into decay, and is resolved into its original invisible gases, and ceases to be an organized body. But the spirit, the soul, is as substantial and as completely organized after it quits the body as it was before; because it is in reality a substance, an enduring immortal creation formed by the Spirit of God from the divine source of all substance and all life. Hence it is written: 'Thou takest away their breath, they die, and return to their dust. Thou sendest forth thy spirit, they are created.'" (Ps. civ. 29, 30.)

St. Paul distinctly teaches that "there is a natural body and there is a spiritual body." The natural body is the one with which the spiritual body clothes itself in this world. Death is simply "shuffling off this mortal coil." It is a withdrawal of the soul or spirit from its earthly dress, its "robe of flesh." As every part of the body is built up and sustained by the spirit, it follows necessarily that the spirit has reproduced its own form. The spiritual eye will see objects in the spiritual world just as the natural eye sees objects in the natural world. And thus with all our faculties and capacities.[1]

The spiritual world is the inner world. It is that which our Lord referred to when he said, "The kingdom of God

---

[1] See Chapter X. for further consideration of this subject.

is within you." When we improve our characters we add something to the spiritual world as truly as we add to a city by building a house. If we become more loving, humble, honest, pure, and truthful, we are helping to create heaven. It is toward this end that all of God's providences are directed, and only with this truth as a key shall we be able to understand his dealings.

CHAPTER VI.

THE PROVIDENTIAL RELATION OF INDIVIDUALS TO HISTORIC EVENTS.

IT is not difficult to recognize an overruling providence in the leading events of history. Even those who have but a dim and shadowy faith in the unseen are wont to freely acknowledge the evidence of a controlling and directing influence by which the currents of human life, as a whole, are mysteriously guided. But their impressions (they can scarcely be called thoughts) are vague and irrational. They express their faith in a *general* providence without stopping to consider that there can be no providential control of events which does not include the smallest and most insignificant details. It would be as reasonable to speak of the general providence of the mainspring of a watch. It is true that the spring furnishes all the power by which the works are kept in motion; but it is equally true that the result aimed at—the measurement of time—depends upon the perfect adjustment and the proper action of every wheel, cog, lever, or whatsoever may stand between the mainspring and the hands. " It is most false, and a mere creature of the reason, to say that the Lord's providence is universal and not at the same time over the minutest particulars; for to provide and govern in the universal, and not at the same time in the least particulars, is not to provide and rule at all. This is philosophically true: and yet it is remarkable that philosophers themselves, even the more distinguished, conceive and think otherwise." [1]

On this point Dr. Bushnell speaks as follows in his work on "Nature and the Supernatural":

"Those who hold to a general and deny a special providence substitute an absurdity for a superstition; for what is a general providence that comprehends no special providence, but a generality made up of no particulars—that is, made up out of nothing? The only intelligent conception is that every event is special, one as truly as another; for nothing comes to pass in God's world without some particular meaning or design. And so the general providence is perfect because the special is complete."

In this, as in so many other religious questions, the truth is obscured and perverted by the false ideas about God. He is thought to bear somewhat the same relation to us that the commander of an army bears to his troops, exercising a general supervision, and leaving the details to be carried out by others. But it should be remembered that an army is a human institution working under all human limitations. The commander would gladly change his general providence to a particular one if he could. In fact, one of the essential qualities of a great commander, that which distinguishes him from his fellow-officers, is his ability to grasp the details of his army and in some measure to control them. The success of the Duke of Wellington was due to this characteristic more than to any other. His knowledge of the condition of his soldiers and of their individual needs was extraordinary. The same was true of Napoleon, who fought his Italian campaign beforehand

---

[1] Swedenborg.

on the map, and nearly every movement was carried out in accordance with the original plan.

The extinction of American slavery is one of the events of history which is often spoken of as providential, and Abraham Lincoln is recognized as an instrument in God's hands for accomplishing it. But how was it done? Was a general edict issued by the Almighty, "Let slavery be extinguished"? Such a conception is impossible. "History is made by individual men as much as a coral reef is made by individual polyps."[1] It was accomplished, as God's plan, through every act of every individual that was in any way related to the final result. Calhoun with his nullification principles, Garrison and his associates with their aggressive efforts, every act of injustice and crime in connection with the Kansas raids, the murder of Lovejoy, the hanging of John Brown, the treachery of government officials, the vacillating character of Buchanan, the vote of every citizen whose ticket helped to elect Lincoln—in short, *all* the acts of all the people who were in the most remote and indirect way connected with the event were instruments in God's hands in shaping the great final issue, which he had planned from the beginning. He did not plan the evil acts of evil men, but he used them. During one of the darkest periods of the war President Lincoln wrote in his diary as follows: "It is quite possible that God's purpose in this war is something different from the purpose of either party, and yet the human instrumentalities, working just as they do, are of the best adaptation to effect his purpose."

Let us take, as another illustration, the Norman invasion. We now see this to have been necessary as a means of

[1] John Fiske.

preparing the English race for its great mission in the world. Did God ordain it as a general purpose, to be ruthlessly carried out regardless of the suffering it would cause? No, this is inconceivable. God is love. He is wisdom. He is infinite. His plan took into account every experience of every individual whose life was affected by the invasion. Homes were broken up, thousands were thrown into servitude, the conquered Saxons were subjected to every form of injustice and cruelty. Yet not a single individual was overlooked or forgotten. God heard with divine compassion every sigh and groan, and overruled every sad experience for the highest good of each and all as far as they would permit.. We may forget the lower orders of the people, the so-called "inferior races," but most assuredly God does not. He distinctly says in his Word that he is no respecter of persons; that his ways are equal, and it is *our* ways that are unequal.

As the thought of a general providence is so deeply rooted in our minds, it may be well to consider one more illustration. In the history of our Civil War the arrival of the "Monitor" in Norfolk Harbor at precisely the right moment to check the depredations of the "Merrimac" made a strong impression upon the public as a remarkable providential event. Had the "Merrimac" succeeded in leaving the harbor, the whole American coast would have been at her mercy, the defenses of our cities being inadequate to serve as a protection from such a novel antagonist. The destruction of a few Northern cities would have led to a recognition of the Southern confederacy by the European nations, and the course of American history would have been completely changed. It was not God's will that this should be allowed. How was it prevented?

The fertile brain of Ericsson had been occupied for years with the problem of devising a craft which should be navigable and formidable, and at the same time afford a minimum of exposure to the attacks of an enemy. At last it took shape in this unique structure. It was completed at the Delemater iron works about a week before the occurrence of the famous "duel." A double set of men were employed upon it, working day and night, although there was no knowledge of the special danger which threatened the safety of the nation at that particular time. The night foreman of that department was so exhausted by the incessant labor that on leaving the works each morning he staggered like a drunken man, and on one occasion he came near being arrested for intoxication while passing along the street. After a time the work was completed as a result of the combined efforts of Mr. Ericsson, the foreman, and the workmen who performed the labor under their direction. The factors involved in the operation were: (1) the genius of Ericsson, (2) the skill and faithfulness of the foreman, and (3) the muscular exertions of the workmen. Mr. Ericsson acted in accordance with the powers of invention, combined with indomitable energy, with which he was endowed. The foreman possessed some qualities which had raised him above his fellow-workmen and enabled him to direct and control them. The others, it may be supposed, worked for so much a day, with no interest beyond that of earning their wages. Each exercised his own will in his own way, and yet above them all was the will and purpose of God that the "Monitor" should reach her destination in time to save the American republic.

And thus it is with all the critical periods and famous

turning-points of history. We see the startling consummation and call it "providential." The real providence is in all the events which have led up to it, including the most insignificant acts of the most obscure individuals. "Oh that night or Blücher would come!" said Wellington at Waterloo. A stupid guide, an order miscarried or misunderstood, a thousand trifling things might have prevented him, but it was not so to be. God's plans never miscarry. Blücher arrives at the right moment, Napoleon is banished to St. Helena, the equilibrium of Europe is restored, and a new chapter begins in the evolution of the nations.

Mr. John Codman Ropes, in a volume entitled "The Campaign of Waterloo," gives so striking a confirmation of the providential side of this event that it might seem almost like a special plea. Yet it is merely the impartial judgment of a historian. His statement of the case may be summarized as follows:

The best military writers agree that the campaign of Waterloo was one of Napoleon's masterpieces. Why did it not succeed?

1. Ney failed to carry out Napoleon's instructions at Quatre Bras. The reason for his course is not known. If he had followed the program as laid down, the campaign would have ended on the 16th (of June) as a triumph for the French, and there could not have been a battle of Waterloo.

2. Napoleon for some unaccountable reason delayed joining Ney on the 17th, and failed to promptly follow up Blücher and the retreating Prussians.

3. Ney's conduct was still more incomprehensible on the 17th in allowing Wellington to retire toward Brussels in good order.

4. Grouchy, without reason, permitted the allied armies to unite. He could have intercepted the Prussians, but perversely failed to do so even after hearing the roar of the artillery, and in spite of the earnest entreaties of Gérard, his corps commander.

The unaccountable course of events leads the historian to say: "It would seem that the very stars in their courses fought against Napoleon. If ever a commander was conquered by fate rather than by his opponents, Napoleon was, in the battle of Waterloo."

CHAPTER VII.

A DIVINE PLAN FOR EVERY LIFE.

WHAT does this mean? Are we only puppets in the hand of some superior power? Is our supposed freedom of action a delusion?

Evolution, as God's method of creating and training an order of immortal beings, intelligent and responsible, with the individuality which responsibility alone can bring, is a rational solution of this problem.

No argument is necessary to prove our freedom of action. It is a part of human consciousness. Every one knows that he can raise his arm, that he can move it to the right or the left, that he can commit a crime or resist the impulse or temptation to commit one. This consciousness has had much influence in confirming the belief in an external God. Since men could exercise a personal will and a personal control of their acts, it has seemed to them that they must be entirely separate from God. Science shows this to be impossible. There have been many curious questions and metaphysical discussions as to what an omnipotent and omnipresent Being could or could not do. The one thing that it would be impossible for God to do is just what the world has generally supposed he does do; namely, separate himself from the objects of his creation. We now see that the *creative* force is no less a *sustaining* force. "By him all things consist," or "hold together," as the revised version renders it in the margin. "In him we live, and move, and have our being." These expressions in the divine Word were formerly accepted only as authoritative statements. We now have in the theory or doctrine of an immanent God a scientific basis for all such statements. We can realize that if God should remove himself from us we would no longer "consist," or "hold together." We would have no "being."

The actual condition has already been indicated in the previous discussions. We are not separated from God, which is impossible, but we are, so to speak, *secluded* from him. We are so inclosed by our material environment that our relation to the divine has become an unconscious relation. This is the only conceivable condition in which we could be left free to *choose* the divine. Having this privilege of choosing, which necessarily implies or carries with it the privilege of rejecting, we have God's magnificent scheme for building character; for creating an order of beings to whose original capacities and powers may be added, by their own free choice, that divine life which is the essence of immortality. "Mere post-mortem consciousness is not immortality."

If such be our relation to God that we have our existence momentarily from him, it follows inevitably that we must be allied in some way to his plans and purposes. There is no escaping this conclusion. Yet it is a result of our imperfect human nature that we do try to escape the conclusion. We revolt against the blessed truth. We discourse with an air of wisdom on "fatalism," and rob ourselves of belief in a Heavenly Father's care by a puny argument. "If it is God's plan that is being carried out instead of ours, then we are not responsible."

But where do we read in the divine Word that God's plan will be carried out *instead* of ours? Are we not, on the contrary, always assured that God's plan will be carried out *through* ours, either for good or evil? " It must needs be that offenses come, but woe unto him through whom the offense cometh." " They hated me without a cause, *that it might be fulfilled which was written.*"

" The troubles which wicked men have caused are recognized by the prophetic souls of the Bible as divinely sent. Envy and greed in Joseph's brethren sell Joseph into Egypt; but when, in after years, Joseph meets his brethren, he reassures them with the words ' Be not grieved nor angry with yourselves that ye sold me hither, for God did send me before you to preserve life.' And in Gethsemane, though the treachery of Judas and the malignity of Caiaphas and the cowardice of Pilate have mingled the cup which is pressed to Christ's lips, he says to Peter, ' The cup which my Father giveth me, shall I not drink it?' "[1]

The moment has arrived in the evolution of human thought when every individual has the privilege of interpreting the laws of Divine Providence in the light afforded by three distinct witnesses: the Word of God, the testimony of science, and the consciousness of the individual.

God's method in his providence is indicated by his method in creation. He creates the atom; with the atom he creates the physical universe. He creates man; with the individual man he builds up the race. This truth leads to simplicity of thought in religious truth. All mysteries are resolved into one infinite mystery—God. " Give me cosmic dust and God, and I will account for all things in the universe," says a devout scientist. But he stopped

[1] The *Outlook*.

one point this side of absolute simplicity. All we need is God. He originates the cosmic dust, and then proceeds to work the creative miracles which follow. Rather, shall we not say that he himself is the only miracle? There are no other miracles, no other mysteries. Matter, attraction, light, heat, all objects, all forces, are but varied manifestations of his power. It is a commonplace remark that there is no greater mystery in the universe than a blade of grass. Yet the principle of life in a blade of grass is no more incomprehensible than the principle of cohesive attraction in the stone that lies beside it. What is life? What is attraction? There is one common answer to both questions—God. This view removes all perplexity with regard to the miracles mentioned in the Scriptures. They are no more difficult to understand and receive than the miracles of nature. "The coming of every little child into the world is an incarnation. The budding of every spring-time is a resurrection. Every year the water is turned into wine by slower but not less marvelous processes than that of Cana of Galilee."[1]

What is the meaning of God's providence in our lives? That depends upon the *object* of our lives. Professor Henry Drummond speaks thus concerning "the end of life":

> What is the end of life? The end of life is not to do good, although many of us think so. It is not to win souls, although I once thought so. The end of life is to do the will of God. That may be in the line of doing good or winning souls, or it may not. For the individual, the answer to the question, What is the end of life? is, To do the will of God, whatever that may be. Spurgeon replied to an invitation to preach to an exceptionally large audience, "I have no ambition to preach to ten thousand people, but to do the will of God," and he declined. If we could have no ambition past the

[1] Rev. J. Hall McIlvaine, D.D.

will of God, our lives would be successful. If we could say, "I have no ambition to go to the heathen, I have no ambition to win souls; my ambition is to do the will of God, whatever that may be," that makes all lives equally great or equally small, because the only great thing in a life is what of God's will there is in it. The maximum achievement of any man's life after it is all over is to have done the will of God.

This is a precious and fundamental truth. Yet we miss the point altogether unless we follow the thought to its logical conclusion. What is God's will concerning each one of us? Is it only a general wish that we shall do right instead of wrong? Assuredly not. It is a *plan*. God has a definite course for each of us to pursue, and to "do his will" is to allow him to lead us by that way instead of following a way of our own. "All we like sheep have gone astray. *We have turned every one to his own way.*" Here it is plainly taught that going astray is not necessarily committing a crime, or following a course of evil; it is simply "turning to our own way."

What a momentous thought is this! My life a plan of God! It is past comprehension. If it is true, the burdens which oppress us should be lifted from our weary souls. We may dismiss the doubts and perplexities that weigh us down, and permit God to lead us by the path which he has chosen for each one of us with infinite wisdom and love. It is too wonderful to believe. It cannot really be true.

It is true if the Bible is true. It is true if science is a credible witness. It is true if the words of Jesus are to be believed. No language could be more clear and unmistakable than that which he employs in speaking of this subject. He foresaw the difficulty that human nature would experience in receiving this doctrine, and therefore guarded it at every point.

"Be not anxious about your life, what you shall eat, or drink, or wear. God takes care of the birds and feeds them from day to day. He bestows upon the common lilies of the field a glory beyond that of Solomon. Wherefore, if God" (not natural law or resident force) "so clothe the grass of the field, which blooms to-day and to-morrow is cast into the oven, shall he not much more clothe you, O ye of little faith? But I know your faith *is* weak, and so I repeat it yet once more, Be not anxious about the things of this world. Your Heavenly Father knows that you need them, and just how far you need them, and if you will give your first thought and care to his kingdom—the kingdom within—he will provide, day by day, the necessities of this earthly life."

Thus, in effect, he addressed his followers, but knowing how hard it was for them and would be for all others to accept this truth, he went on to explain that God's care of us is so minute and particular that he even numbers the hairs of our heads.

Here we have, from the lips of the One whom we accept as our guide for time and for eternity, a clear statement of the doctrine of Divine Providence. We may accept it, or we may reject it, or (which is the usual course) we may profess to accept it and still practically reject it, and thus fail to obtain the peace, comfort, and strength it was intended to impart. But the purport of the instruction is unmistakable. It is supported by numberless other passages in the Scriptures, by the history of God's dealings with the human race, and now, in these later days, by the revelations of science.

It cannot be denied that the doctrine is hard to accept and hard to apply to the complex experiences of life. To learn to accept it against the evidence of our senses and the inclinations of the flesh is the one object for which we are placed in this world—the purpose for which the vast machinery of the universe was created. When we have learned the lesson fully, and have substituted God's will for our own, we are ready to be transferred to the heavenly world whose inhabitants are called "angels" or "messengers," because they have ceased to live for themselves and seek only to know and do the will of the Heavenly Father.

How, in this world of spiritual darkness, are we to know what God's plan is from day to day? Are we to cease planning for ourselves?

By no means. God gave us our faculties and expects us to use them. The faculty of planning is one of the most important of them all. We are told to look at the fowls of the air as an example, and they are admirable planners. They plan a whole season in advance, and provide for the safety and comfort of their little families with surprising forethought and skill. They *plan* but do not *worry*, and it is their trust that we are enjoined to imitate.

In considering God's plans we must never for a moment lose sight of the fact that the end he seeks is our eternal welfare, and not our earthly happiness. He is not indifferent to the latter, but he loves us too well to allow the lower and temporary life to take precedence of the higher and eternal interests. We are at school. The purpose of our being here is that we may learn such lessons as will fit us for the best use of our faculties and endowments in the everlasting hereafter. These faculties and powers are to be trained, disciplined, formed, and directed to wise uses. The experiences which God sends us by his providence day by day have reference only to the development of our spiritual powers. If success and happiness will do our souls the most good (or, in case of our wilful resistance of his plans, the least harm), he will send or permit them. If disappointment, illness, suffering, heart-sickening delay, loss of any kind, will serve a better purpose in the development of our spiritual life, those experiences will be sent, but always with the comforting assurance, "My grace is sufficient for thee."

It is evident, therefore, that God's plan cannot possibly include any wrong-doing, any crookedness, nor even any course in which the right is doubtful. *Doubtful right is wrong*, for it compromises the conscience, which is in all cases an evil. So far, then, our way is clear. We must dismiss from our lives or turn away from any plan or course that includes or involves a swerving from righteousness. To tamper with evil because God has promised to overrule it is not only an insult to his goodness, but also to our own intelligence.

If we believe that God has a plan for us, and try earnestly to follow it, will our way be always plain? No. That would make life too easy. There would be no robust quality in our faith, no real vigor and vitality in the warp and woof of our character if such were the case. It is not by an arbitrary law that we are called in this world to walk by faith and not by sight. It is an essential element in the great process of character-building. To believe that God's hand is guiding us, although we cannot see it or be distinctly conscious of it, is the foundation of true spiritual development. To *believe* that everything depends upon God, and yet *act* as if everything depended upon our own efforts, is the true and only way to establish what may be called a divine individuality in our souls.

The Christian ought not to find a difficulty in such a faith when even the so-called heathen philosophers have proclaimed it. Plato, in his tenth dialogue, declares that "a superior nature of such excellence as the divine shows its superiority by hearing, seeing, and knowing all things, and caring for the smallest things in the world as well as for the greatest." Aristotle wrote: "It is a tradition received from of old, among all men, that God is the creator and preserver of all things, and that nothing in nature is sufficient to its own existence without his superintending protection."

CHAPTER VIII.

DIFFICULTIES CLASSIFIED AND CONSIDERED.

THE difficulties which arise in our minds concerning a universal providence in human lives are nearly all embraced under the following heads:

1. Our insignificance. How can we expect an Infinite Being to be interested in the petty details of our insect lives?

2. Our imperfections. What right have we to believe that God will make himself responsible for our weaknesses and follies?

3. The complex conditions of life. For example, there are two vessels at sea, sailing in opposite directions: how can an impartial providence be adjusted to both?

4. The disorganizing influence of sin. How can God's purposes be carried out with those who set themselves against his will?

These questions will be considered in their order.

I. OUR INSIGNIFICANCE.

This difficulty is entirely of our own creation. Whatever apparent ground for it there may have been under the old idea of an external deity disappears instantly under the illuminating theory of an immanent God. To the infinite there can be no great or small. To an Infinite

Creator who calls all things into existence by the direct exercise of his own being there can be no such gradations as we see or think we see. They are the result of our limited vision. Ruskin says: "We treat God with irreverence by banishing him from our thoughts, not by referring to his will on slight occasions. His is not the finite authority of intelligence which cannot be troubled with small things."

The element of infinity sets at naught all our ideas concerning the relations of things. For instance, it is an axiom in geometry that the arc of a circle cannot be a straight line. Yet the arc of an infinite circle must be a straight line.

In the sight of an Infinite God there can be no such fact or quality as that which we describe as insignificance. Every atom in the physical universe, every sentient being of God's creation in all his myriad worlds, is as fully under his supervision as if there were no other atom, no other being. The fallacy of any argument based upon the idea of our insignificance may be shown by an illustration. We may imagine a tiny plant in the deep recesses of an impenetrable forest where no ray of sunshine has ever penetrated to its lowly bed. Impressed with its own "insignificance," it utters a sad complaint: "It is not possible that the great sun in the sky knows or cares anything about me. The tall trees are worthy of his care, but I am wholly beneath his notice." To this complaint there is one sufficient answer. The sun is the author of its being. It was called into existence and is constantly sustained by the solar light and heat. In reality, therefore, as far as its relation to the sun is concerned, it is no more insignificant than the grandest of the trees by which it is shaded.

Thus it is with each one of us. "Because God is, we are." We exist from moment to moment by the unceasing exercise of his creative power. There is no middle ground between " no God " and an infinite God who cannot be excluded from our lives without excluding life itself. The plea of insignificance is therefore ruled out of the case altogether. In its place should be substituted the vital truth that all God's purposes concerning us are for spiritual ends, and we then see that the things which are outwardly most insignificant may be of the deepest import to our souls. The relation of Divine Providence to our daily lives can only be understood properly when judged by this standard.

In conversation with a Christian friend who expressed her faith in Divine Providence in the usual terms, I said: " Do you believe it is a part of God's plan that we should be talking together at the present moment? " This startled her. She said, " How can it be? You came here because you chose to come, and to carry out certain plans of your own. I did the same." " Suppose we go a little further. Your servant breaks a valuable dish. Do you think God has anything to do with that?" She seemed shocked, and said the idea appeared to her " blasphemous." I find this is a common feeling among Christians when the words of Scripture are carried out to a logical conclusion and applied to every-day occurrences. But what a mistaken impression it is, whether viewed in the light of reason or faith. We say we believe God to be infinite, yet immediately proceed to limit him by shutting him out of a part of our lives. On the other hand, we acknowledge that all grace and strength must come from him, yet doubt his having any connection with the daily experiences through which we must grow if we grow at all. The breaking of a valuable dish *must* have some effect upon the character of the owner. Either she will give way to anger and suffer spiritual harm, or she will control her feelings, master her evil temper, and the loss of a porcelain dish will be for her the means of gaining a heavenly grace. "Better is he that ruleth his spirit than he that taketh a city."

All our acts and experiences in this world have two sides, an external side and a spiritual side. The external side is that which affects our present comfort and happiness, and therefore we are chiefly occupied with it, and are scarcely conscious of the influence it is exerting upon our spiritual nature. But God looks chiefly at the spiritual, and considers the external only in its relation to the "kingdom within." If hunger or cold, or privation of any kind, or physical suffering, or the destruction of our dearest hopes will serve the best purpose in building up the divine life in our souls, we may rest assured that they are what our Heavenly Father will send. Of course it is hard. *It is meant to be.* "No chastening for the present is joyous, but grievous, but *afterward* it bringeth the peaceable fruits of righteousness." God's infinite wisdom is nowhere more apparent than in the marvelous discernment with which he detects our special weakness and sends the shaft of suffering where our natures feel most keenly. With our limited knowledge of ourselves we could not have imagined a combination of circumstances in which we could be made to suffer so deeply. Is God unkind in this? No. When we look back from "the other side" we shall see that not one pang could be spared. Each stroke is essential to the completion of the work. And then how grateful we shall be to our Heavenly Father for persevering without regard to our ignorant prayers for relief, and for holding us with his loving yet unyielding hand in the furnace of affliction till the purpose of the discipline is attained. Since he takes such infinite pains with us, using all the trifling occurrences of our lives (if we will so permit) in building up our characters "till Christ be formed in us," we may be sure that, whatever arguments may be adduced against the universality of Divine Providence, our insignificance is not one of them.

2. OUR IMPERFECTIONS.

What of them? They are the stuff out of which we are to be made. "Best men are molded out of faults." A self-indulgent David becomes the world's model for penitence and humility. A vacillating Peter, "unstable as water," is transformed into a rock against which trials and temptations spend their force in vain. Saul the persecutor furnishes the material for Paul the martyr. To rule our imperfections out of the problem of Divine Providence would amount to ruling ourselves out, for we are merely a grand sum total of imperfections. "But I am dull and stupid, as well as sinful. I make no end of discouraging blunders. Can I expect God to overrule my imbecility?" Well, it is just what he has promised to do. When his promises were given to us it was with a complete knowledge of our imperfections and weaknesses, and of all that was involved in them. Our Heavenly Father intended them to be factors in our development. *But they were given us to be overcome, and not to be yielded to.* Speaking once with a Christian friend of one who possessed excellent gifts, but was strongly tempted by an inherited "inertia" to leave them unemployed and undeveloped, my friend said quizzically, " Don't you think God makes lazy folks?" Undoubtedly he does, for he makes everybody; but it was intended that this infirmity, like all others, should be resisted and overcome. Judas, with his keen business instincts, might have become the honored treasurer of the infant church if he had ruled his passion instead of allowing himself to be ruled by it. Tennyson gives us the law for our imperfections when he says that

> Men may rise on stepping-stones
> Of their dead selves to higher things.

Our infirmities are obstacles which may be transformed into stepping-stones. But they must be sacrificed. They must be changed from masters to servants. If yielded to, they are our deadly enemies. If conquered, they are turned into messengers of good to our souls.

This struggle with imperfection and sin constitutes a large share of the "warfare" that is so often spoken of in the Bible. We must not be deceived by the great truth that salvation is God's gift. Canaan was God's gift to the children of Israel, yet they were obliged to fight for every inch of the territory, and to overcome and drive out all the native inhabitants. They made the mistake of compromising with some of the tribes instead of exterminating them, which led to endless trouble and misery in their after history. "Which things are an allegory." We may not excuse or palliate any of our weaknesses, but must conquer them all in the name of the Lord.

In this battle of life we have the clear and unmistakable promise of God's sympathy and help. Far more than this, he even engages to fight the battles for us. Knowing our utter incapacity to gain the victory in our own strength, Jesus, our human friend and divine Saviour, asks us to cast all our care on him, promising to bear our burdens and overcome our enemies. Could infinite love go further than this?

3. THE COMPLEX CONDITIONS OF LIFE.

The infinity of God, our Father and friend, ought to be a sufficient answer to this objection. As an illustration of his boundless power we have only to look at the vast complications of the stellar universe. Each world is held in its appointed orbit, though attracted in every direction by myriads of other worlds. Consider also the perfect balance of the vast mass of waters that encircle our earth. If the rotary motion of the globe should be quickened only so slightly as to make a difference of one minute in the length of our day, it is calculated that the ocean would be rolled up at the equator to the depth of 169 miles.

But it may be objected that the stars and the ocean are passive objects, while we have separate and opposing wills of our own. Does not this prevent even an Infinite Being from carrying out his purposes concerning us? In certain respects it does, unquestionably. God's wish for us is that we may be happy. Since all human beings have a capacity for the enjoyments of heaven, it may be said in that sense that all are foreordained or predestinated for heaven. But that beneficent plan of the Heavenly Father is prevented by the wilfulness of those who prefer their own ways to his ways, and thus shut themselves out of heaven. What then? Does God let us alone? No. His love is persistent and insistent. Having rejected the best, he puts before us the next possible good, and after that the next, and thus till every possibility is exhausted. George Macdonald says: "Those who will not consent to be living stones in God's temple may have to be ground into mortar for it."

The power of Divine Providence in controlling the complex affairs of human life may be illustrated by the telegraph. When first invented it was thought necessary to have two wires, one for the outgoing and the other for the returning current. That limitation was soon outgrown, and now it is found possible to send several messages both ways at the same time. How it is done is entirely beyond our comprehension. In some mysterious way the electric currents do our bidding without interfering with each other. If such miracles are possible in the physical world, it ought not to be difficult to believe that God's control of human affairs is perfect and all-inclusive, however complex and conflicting they may appear to us.

But we need to remind ourselves constantly that it is our spiritual and not our temporal well-being that our Heavenly Father is seeking to compass. A friend once said to me: "I ought to believe in special providences." (The old misleading term!) "I know of a most remarkable case. A friend of mine was going from Chicago to New York to take a steamer for Europe. He was detained on his way to the train, and missed it. By that means he missed the steamer. The train he intended to take was wrecked, and a number of people were killed and injured, and the steamer on which he would have sailed was never heard from." "But," said I, "what about the people who were allowed to take the train and to depart on the steamer? What was the providence in their case?"

"Oh," he replied, "I'm not considering that side of the question now." Inasmuch as the disastrous side is usually thus ignored, it is remarkable that the subject of Divine Providence has not fallen into utter contempt among men. That it has not done so shows how strong is the instinct in human nature to believe in an overruling Power. The demand of our hearts for such an object of faith is so imperative that we cling to it even against the laws of reason and justice.

A rational and satisfactory solution of such difficulties can only be found by introducing the element of eternity as a factor in the problem. The final and permanent good of each individual is the end sought, and not the comfort and happiness of these few fleeting moments. It is just as much a providence that some shall be permitted to go into danger, injury, and death as that others shall be guarded and withheld from such experiences. Each is led in the way that an all-wise Father sees to be best. To some, the time for translation to the other world has come, and they pass over through accident instead of disease. To others the discipline of bodily suffering is seen to be necessary, and that is sent in its season.

If this doctrine seems hard, let it be compared for a moment with the alternative of inexorable laws without a loving Father to overrule them for the good of his children. Hear what John Stuart Mill says of the tenderness of nature:

"In sober truth, nearly all the things that men are hanged or imprisoned for doing are nature's every-day performances. Nature impales men, breaks them as if on the wheel, throws them to wild beasts, burns them, crushes them to death like the first Christian martyr, starves them, freezes them, poisons them by the quick or slow venom of her exhalations, and has hundreds of other hideous deaths in reserve, such as the ingenious cruelty of a Domitian or a Torquemada never surpassed. Everything, in short, which the worst men commit either against life or property is committed on a larger scale by natural agents."

All this being true, what can save us from sinking down in hopeless despair? Nothing but the message God has sent us out of heaven assuring us that nature's forces are *his* forces, and that he is using them to discipline and train us, being willing that we should suffer a little while in this world in order that we may be prepared for eternal happiness in the world to come.

> One adequate support
> For the calamities of mortal life
> Exists, one only: an assured belief
> That the procession of our fate, howe'er
> Sad or disturbed, is ordered by a Being
> Of infinite benevolence and power,
> Whose everlasting purposes embrace
> All accidents, converting them to good.[1]

If we refuse to take our discipline in the right way, alas for us! The one thing that God will not do is to *force* us into submission. He must have children, and not slaves. Those who go down the dark ways of death are slaves, but the chains they wear are of their own forging.

4. OUR SINFULNESS.

In considering this topic we must keep distinctly in mind its relation to our general subject. We are not called upon to discuss the origin of sin, its nature, or its

---
[1] Wordsworth.

punishment, but simply its relation to the rulings of Divine Providence in human events. Sin is here, and all philosophers and moralists agree that it is here by necessity. There can be no sunlight without shadow. There can be no good without a possible corresponding evil. Right without a contingent wrong would be a nerveless, characterless negative. Sin is opposition to God's will. Does it not therefore thwart that will? I am a sinful creature. Does not this fact throw me out of the current and purpose of Divine Providence?

What answer does revelation give to this question? "He causeth the wrath of man to praise him, and the remainder of wrath he will restrain." If this means anything, it means that there are no acts of wickedness in the world but those which God permits for some wise purpose. The most casual glance at past or contemporaneous history will show how wonderfully the lives and labors of wicked and selfish men are used in the furtherance of God's beneficent plans. Take a single illustration. It is his will and purpose that the gospel shall be carried to the uttermost parts of the earth. For the accomplishment of this result it is necessary that railways shall be built, lines of steamships established, and other great enterprises carried on. By whom is this important work done? Is it undertaken by earnest Christian men for a Christian or benevolent purpose? Very rarely. In almost every instance the ruling motive-power of those great enterprises is selfishness and ambition. T. S. Arthur, writing on this subject, says:

"The strongest impelling forces at this day are love of self and love of the world, manifesting themselves in ambition, desire to rule, to be greatest, richest, most honored.

These are the forces that move the wonderful and complicated machinery of government, trade, commerce, and organized industries; and only the Infinite Wisdom can restrain and direct the fiery impulses and struggling antagonisms thus set in motion, and out of individual self-seeking evolve the best results for all."

The question which appeals to every erring child of God is this: "Can my sins by any possibility be made a part of the divine plan?" Beyond a doubt they can be and are. If God can make the wrath of wicked men to praise him, it is certain that he can overrule the wrong-doing of those who are trying, however imperfectly, to serve him. Let the reader recall his own experience. As we look back upon our lives, can we not see that certain elements of character have resulted from our being allowed to fall into sin which apparently could not have been gained in any other way? We deplore the sin, but how can we be otherwise than grateful for the marvelous grace which brought good to our souls out of it? To wicked or worldly people sin may be a luxury. To the Christian it is a whip of scorpions. How crushed and humiliated he feels as he looks back upon the temptation yielded to, the sin committed. No room for self-righteousness now. The only hope is in fleeing to him who was bruised for our iniquities and chastened for the purchase of our peace. With his stripes we may be healed if we will bow before him with penitence and a sincere sorrow for our sin. But we should go to him as a friend, and not as an enemy. "The mark which God sets upon Cain is for his protection. Our sin is forever the burden of his care. In our madness he patiently awaits the sane thought and purpose."[1]

[1] "God in His World."

I think this may be accepted as a spiritual axiom:

Anything that increases our sense of dependence upon God, and drives or draws us nearer to him, is a blessing, whether it be sickness, sorrow, loss, or repentance.

The question may be asked, Is there not danger in this doctrine? Will not some be tempted to yield to sin by the thought that God will afterward condone it? To this the answer may be given most emphatically, No. He who would make such a use of God's mercy shows himself by that token to be already a child of hell. He is seeking excuses for sin, and will find them at all hazard. He is the man with a muck-rake, grubbing for filth, and we may be sure he will not be contented unless he is wallowing in it.

With what more fitting words can this chapter be closed than the following, written six hundred years ago by the saintly Tauler:

"The very least and the very greatest sorrows that God ever suffers to befall thee proceed from the depths of his unspeakable love; and such great love were better for thee than the highest and best gifts besides that he has given thee, or ever could give thee, if thou couldst but see it in this light. So that if your little finger only aches, if you are cold, if you are hungry or thirsty, if others vex you by their words or deeds, or whatever happens to you that causes you distress or pain, it will all help to fit you for a noble and blessed state."

CHAPTER IX.

OUR FATHER'S PLAN FOR EACH AND ALL.

WHO can still the questionings of the human heart? Who can satisfy the desire of every child of earth to know

> . . . by what power, without our own consent,
> Caught in this snare of life we know not how,
> We were placed here to suffer and to sin,
> To be in misery, we know not why.

We have a constant and painful sense of defeat. The circumstances of life seem arranged for our discomfiture. Jacob's agonizing cry, "All these things are against me," is the voice of universal human nature under the sharp and pitiless discipline of life. We seem so left to ourselves, as if no one knew and no one cared. The condition is thus graphically described by George Mac Donald:

"To trust in spite of the look of being forsaken, to keep crying out into the vast, whence comes no returning voice, and where seems no hearing, to see the machinery of the world pauselessly grinding on as if self-moved, caring for no life, nor shifting a hair's-breadth for all entreaty, and yet believe that God is awake and utterly loving; to desire nothing but what comes meant for us from his hand; to wait patiently, ready to die of hunger, fearing only lest faith should fail—such is the victory that overcometh the world, such is faith indeed."

A key to the difficult problem of life is furnished by the single word "eternity." The Infinite Creator is a loving Father who sends his children to school in the material world as a way of preparing them for the spiritual world. The material world is not an end but a means. Life here is not life in a full sense of the word: it is a preparation for life. If we have a sense of defeat, it is just what we were meant to have. Not to be defeated in this world is a sign of defeat in the world to come. We can only gain the other world by losing this. Our Father's plan embraces both worlds, but the material world is only used for our creation, discipline, shaping, and in all things making us ready for the world of realities—the eternal life.

Since God is infinite, what must his plan for us include? Everything. No smallest influence which may in any way affect our character can be left out. It is a strange fatuity which leads Christian believers to doubt God's attention to small things because of his infinity. It is his infinity which makes it impossible for any factor, however minute, to be overlooked. Any omission of the slightest detail would make him less than infinite. There would be something that infinity did not include—an inconceivable thought.

As it is so difficult to accept this truth against the evidence of our senses, let us follow it out to the last detail of human experience, and consider it in its application to the various stages of life. The first topic that claims our attention is

HEREDITY.

When does a human being begin to be made? Dr. Oliver Wendell Holmes says, with quite as much wisdom as wit, that a child's training should begin a hundred years before it is born. If we take into account the vast complication of ancestral influences which contribute to the character of every individual of the race, we begin to form some conception of the infinitude of the Being who controls those influences and leads them to a prescribed ultimation. " But these influences all act in accordance with a general law," it is said. True. But God made the law, as science assures us. He is the law. Nothing can exist without him. "If I make my bed in hell, behold, he is there." If a Divine Providence controls our lives, it controlled equally the lives of those who came before us, and whose characters helped to form ours. We must accept heredity, like everything else we possess, as coming from our Heavenly Father's hands. We may deplore some angularity or infirmity, or a physical weakness which causes us to "ache where our mother ached half a century ago," but we are not to repine as if God had nothing to do with it. It is true that we are handicapped, that we are weighted and hampered by disabilities for which we are not responsible. But God knows it and has provided for it. Out of these various strands, some bright, some dark, he will weave his perfect pattern if we will submit ourselves in loving faith to his wise guidance.

EARLY ENVIRONMENT.

The circumstances which surround us in childhood have such unlimited power in forming our characters and shaping our destinies that it is very difficult for us to accept without murmuring certain untoward influences which were permitted to come into our lives. We see plainly in reviewing the past that temptations were allowed to assault us in childhood or youth which either led to bitter struggles or to great evils—often to both. "If God is watching over us every moment, why could not this allurement have been warded off?" Because it was needed to develop a certain side of your character. "But it appealed to my weakest side. I could have resisted a much greater temptation at some other point." This shows that you needed strengthening just there, and the moral qualities, like all others, can only be strengthened by exercise, trial, and testing. "Alas! in this case I was not strengthened, but weakened. I yielded to the temptation and followed evil ways a long time." Yes, but God is not done with you yet. He is still at work. The penitence you now feel is a part of his plan. Do not waste time and strength in vain regrets over an irrevocable past. We may be the creatures of yesterday, but we are the creators of to-morrow. In your rebound from those evils God foresaw that you could reach a higher moral elevation than you could have attained without that sad experience. His love and wisdom are combined to lead us to the highest good of which we are capable. Nothing but our persistent wilfulness can defeat his beneficent plan for our ultimate happiness.

EDUCATION.

Of all things in this world a good education is one of the most important. But it is necessary to realize just what is or should be meant by "a good education." Dr. T. T. Munger says: "The object of education is not to teach us how to get a living, but to teach us how to live." Taking the word "live" in its broadest sense, this definition should bring comfort to those who have occasion to regret a lack of scholarship. Scholarship is desirable, but it is not the only education. The Duke of Wellington said: " Educate men without religion and you but make them clever devils." God's plan for our education is to develop the spiritual nature. The intellectual faculties are of secondary importance when measured by the scale of eternal life. For the promotion of that life God makes use of all our earthly experiences, and is as willing to sacrifice our education as our fortune if the sacrifice will do the most to build up our spiritual nature. It therefore goes without saying that the degree of our intellectual training is a mere incident in the divine, eternal plan. Every one should obtain the best "education" he possibly can, but those who believe in a Heavenly Father's care will not fret and chafe over opportunities that are denied them, but will strive to enter into the divine plan for their development, which must be better than any they had formed for themselves. It may be painfully evident that our lack of certain elements of culture is a constant hindrance to our getting ahead in our earthly plans and business. But that is not necessarily a misfortune. Getting ahead in this world too often means getting behind in the world to come. We cannot be sufficiently grateful for the love which is willing to save us from sacrificing our eternal interests for those which are merely temporal and fleeting.

OCCUPATION OR BUSINESS.

The selection of our life-work is a serious and oftentimes a most perplexing question. It may be difficult to decide what business we are best fitted for. Or we may have a decided talent in a certain direction and no way opens for its exercise. How comforting is the faith that God has planned and arranged it all, and we have only to follow his plan day by day. "Ah! how gladly would I do this," is the cry of many a weary soul, "if I could but know what his plan is." Is this your case, dear friend? Then one element of the divine plan is evident at first sight—the development of your faith. Perhaps your special prayer has been that your faith might be strengthened. How have you expected that prayer to be answered? Have you imagined that God kept some elixir of faith in a bottle which he would administer to you in response to your entreaties? It would seem that many have some such idea. There is but one way in which our faith can be strengthened, and that is by its exercise, and the only way in which it can be exercised is by depriving us of the things of sight and sense upon which we would naturally lean. This leaves us in a condition of uncertainty. Having no earthly foundation on which to build, we are forced to look elsewhere for a foundation. "Other refuge have I none" is not merely the expression of a religious experience. It applies equally to all the ways of life. But, with the perversity of the human heart, we rarely apply the truth to our business or what we are wont to call "worldly affairs" unless compelled to do so by the failure of our own efforts.

There are few things more misleading and harmful than the common idea that worldly matters are separate and apart from the religious life. Satan, in all his long and successful career, never devised a shrewder plan than that of leading Christians to make a distinction between religion and business, between sacred and secular affairs. We may have special periods for devotion, but religion, whether we wish it or not, enters into every act of our lives. "Other world?" says Emerson; "there is no other world. Here or nowhere is the eternal fact." The readiness with which the church has allowed itself to be caught in this snare is amazing. The Scriptures give no possible warrant for such a notion. They teach us that "whether we eat or drink, or whatever we do, we should do all for the glory of God." This plainly implies that in all things we must either act for the glory of God or for the opposite. There is no neutral ground. To eat and drink temperately in grateful acknowledgment of our indebtedness to God for his gifts is doing it to his glory. To eat and drink for the gratification of the senses, with no recognition of a Father's love in providing the bounties, is ministering to self and serving the devil. The Bible standard is not a doubtful one. In all our relations to our fellow-men we must either obey the law of love or the opposite. To quote Emerson again: "Every man takes good care that his neighbor shall not cheat him. After a time he begins to be concerned lest he cheat his neighbor. Then all goes well. His market cart becomes a chariot of the sun."

The law of service is universal whether we will it to be so or not. As we ride along in a luxurious railway coach, we are profiting by the labor of all who helped to build the road or construct the coach. We should lift our hat to the working-man with his shovel, for without him we would be making our journey in the stage-coach of the past. There is an equal dignity in all useful callings. The preacher in his pulpit, the professor in his class-room, the author in his library, have no spiritual rights above the grocer or the day-laborer. It is open to our common humanity in every grade and condition

> To feel, through all this fleshly dress,
> Bright shoots of everlastingness.

No other law than this could serve as a basis for the operations of a universal providence. In truth, it is by the law of Divine Providence that the condition of equality is created. This equality extends not only to all individuals but to all events. "There is no great or small" is a truth of universal application. The sale of a pound of tea is one with the transfer of a kingdom. The motive behind it determines its character and value in either case.

Thus it is that there are no earthly affairs. There is a spiritual quality in every act of our lives. It leads toward heaven or it leads toward hell. Nothing could be more pernicious or benumbing than the idea that some of our actions occupy a sort of middle ground and have no practical relation to our spiritual life. One of the many unfortunate consequences of this error is a loss of faith in Divine Providence. It excludes God from our daily business, where, in truth, we need him most. Such a false idea should be banished from our minds forever. God is a silent partner in every legitimate and honest business. His providence extends to the smallest transactions. Those who adopt crooked or doubtful business methods not only exclude the Divine Providence, but they open the door to the great enemy, who will be sure to step in and take the direction of affairs. His first object will be to convince the other members of the firm that religion and business must be carefully separated. They may be as pious as they please on Sundays if they will but follow his maxims the other six days of the week.

SUCCESS.

Having chosen a business or occupation, it is right to do all in our power (along the line of uprightness, and with due regard to the law of love for God and our fellow-men) to make it a success. But in doing this, the Christian must not forget that we have a Divine Partner whose standard of success is entirely different from ours, and whose judgment should be accepted as final in this and in all matters. He understands the whole case; we know but a small part of it. He sees our inward needs; of these we are mostly ignorant. He plans for eternity; we can plan only with reference to our earthly conditions and surroundings. In a word, while we are aiming at success in business, God is planning for our success in life, and if the sacrifice of the former is essential to the interests of the latter, it is to be expected that the sacrifice will certainly be made. But we are by no means to assume that this is necessary. On the contrary, the fact of being led, after careful and prayerful consideration, to adopt a certain calling, is at least partial evidence that we are meant to succeed in it. We may hope that prosperity is intended for us, and that we shall have grace to make a wise use of it. But there is a world-wide, an eternity-wide difference between a business that is consecrated to God and one that is not. In the former case prosperity will not dazzle and ruin, nor adversity lead to despair. But a business that is not consecrated to God and the service of our fellow-men cannot be wholesome or sound in any of its relations. God will overrule it as he does all other things that are wrong or disorderly. But it is not, and cannot be, to the one that conducts it, a blessing in the sense in which our Heavenly Father desires to bless us in business.

In order to reach the lowest foundation-stone of this subject of business it is necessary to discuss, as a separate point, the question of

MONEY.

Here is a test of faith. The mind revolts against the idea that God has anything to do with the money question. Of all things, it seems the least worthy of his notice. This, too, is one of Satan's devices. Whatever we keep God out of, we make room for Satan to get into. If he could gain entire control of the money question, he could well afford to let all other things go. It takes but little consideration to show the fallacy of our views on this subject. If there is a Divine Providence directing any portion of our affairs, it ought to have not less but more to do with money than with anything else, for money represents nearly all other things. But there is no distinction in the divine supervision. God's plan includes the pocket-book and the bank-account. He knows exactly how much money it is best for us to have, down to the last farthing. It is very difficult for the successful business man, in the church or out of it, to believe this. Can he not trace his prosperity directly to his own industry, his own frugality, his own sagacity and shrewdness? There is his neighbor who made such a bad investment and lost so many thousands of dollars. The folly of that move was evident to him from the beginning. It is because *he* has had the sense to keep clear of such ventures that he has succeeded where others have failed.

This is a pleasant line of argument for the prosperous man, but it is neither sound nor true. Many others with equal industry, frugality, and sagacity have tried and failed. Something was wrong. The business location was not favorable. A partnership did not prove fortunate. The failure of other houses brought unavoidable ruin. Health failed just as success was within easy reach. These are the apparent reasons. They are the real reasons, but they were the means used by God to prevent a success which he saw would not be best in this case.

There is another flaw in the prosperous man's argument. His industry and frugality produce success up to a certain point, and then the tide suddenly turns. It is very mysterious. The means and methods which once worked so smoothly now produce the opposite effect from what they did before. Losses come where gains were formerly certain. The judgment, the prevision, the skill, are the same, but the results do not follow. This is by no means a rare experience. The only way of safety and of true welfare in money matters, as in all others, is to accept God's plan for them. Before doing this we must first believe that he has a plan. That plan must include a consecration of our money, as of ourselves. In this spirit we may go forward with perfect trust. If business prospers and large means are given, wisdom will not be wanting to direct in the use of them. If the income is small, or if, as Mac Donald says, we are compelled to "burn in the slow fire of poverty," the heart will not be crushed, though it may be sorely tried. When our Lord came to redeem the world he chose to take his place among the poorest of the earth. What greater privilege can there be than to share his lot, although, like all other forms of discipline, for the present "it is not joyous but grievous"?

HEALTH.

There are many in these days who say that sickness is disorderly, unnecessary, and not a part of God's plan. There is a sense in which all this is true, no doubt. But disease is here, nevertheless, and it has had an important part in the formation of many lovely Christian characters. It has been a potent factor in the lives of not a few of the Christian poets who "learned in suffering what they taught in song." To do all in our power to win health and to keep it is as much a duty as to be honest. We cannot "present our bodies as a *living* sacrifice" if they are half devitalized by disease. Yet, when we have done all we can, if sickness and pain are still our portion, we have the comfort of knowing that our Lord, our Father, the Wonderful, the Counselor, the Physician of our souls, will overrule and bless the sufferings of our bodies, as he does all other human ills. With divine skill and compassion he makes them a part of the "all things" which are promised to "work together for our good." Not a thrill of pain will be permitted that will not help to refine our spirits and increase our capacity for eternal life, if we will but accept each trial as from him.

USEFULNESS.

When self-love is driven out of one stronghold of the human heart, it straightway tries to get possession of another. "Self comes to life in the slaying of self." The very last refuge from which it has to be dislodged is our *usefulness*. Surely we ought to strive to be useful. If we do so, earnestly and faithfully, we have a right to expect God's blessing on our efforts. Especially is this true if our work is that of "winning souls." Such is our natural feeling. But it is possible to make as great a mistake in this direction as in any other. One of the most useful utterances of this generation is that of Professor Drum mond: "The end of life is not to do good. It is not to win souls, although I once thought so. It is to do the will of God." There is at the present day a great amount of what may be called "busybody religion." "Many run to and fro, but knowledge is not increased." Strenuous efforts are made to "save souls" by those who have not yet learned the fundamental principles of Christian living. Many who are undoubtedly sincere Christians, and are leading consecrated lives, make a great mistake in the direction of their activities. Some of the methods of Christian work, which were legitimate and useful in the past, are not suitable to the conditions of the present. In this day, which is characterized by a wide diffusion of light and knowledge, it would be strange if religious methods were not more or less changed. Dwight L. Moody, the most successful revivalist of the age, recognizes this truth and gives it a forcible expression in these words: "There is something better than a revival of religion, and that is a religion that doesn't need to be revived."

We have no call to feel anxious about our usefulness. God made us, and he knows exactly what he wants us to do. Perhaps it is to *do* nothing, but only to *be*. Perhaps it is to exemplify patience under the thwarting of our plans of usefulness. There is a great deal said in the Bible about *waiting* on the Lord, but very little about *working* for him. The reason for this is obvious. If we will wait on him—that is, look to see what his will is concerning us —we shall always know what he wants us to do. It has been illustrated in this way: Suppose the master of a large household employs a man and tells him that his service is to sit in a certain chair and answer a certain bell when it rings. He waits a long time without receiving a summons.

Many others are about, engaged busily in various ways. At last he begins to feel that he has no right to be idle. He leaves his place of waiting and joins the others in their work. After a time the bell rings, but he is not there to answer it. He is in another part of the house, "serving his master," as he thinks, but he is doing no such thing. He is interfering seriously with his master's plans, for the work he was summoned to do was more important than all the rest, and now it is spoiled because he was a busybody instead of a faithful servant. God has given a beautiful lesson on this subject in the scriptural history of David. David was anxious to build a temple "unto the name of the Lord God." But he was forbidden by God to do it, "because of the wars which were about him on every side." But this message was sent for his comfort: "Whereas it was in thine heart to build an house unto my name, thou didst well that it was in thine heart." That is to say, the purpose was fully accepted although it was not carried out.

It is not easy to learn the lesson of waiting for our work and leaving it wholly in the Lord's hands. A minister prepares a sermon with special care, hoping to reach the heart of some individuals for whom he feels a deep concern. He labors long and prays much over it. Sunday comes and proves to be a day of storm. Not one of those for whom he wrote the sermon is present. He is discouraged and downhearted. Did God forget this time? Is he indifferent? Does he care any less than you do for those precious souls? No. It is a time for you to trust, and to trust fully and cheerfully. The story is a familiar one of a minister preaching to a congregation consisting of a single individual, and that it was only after many years that he learned of the person's conversion as a result of that sermon. Suppose he had never heard of it? This would make no difference. We are to sow. God will attend to the harvest in his own time and way.

LIVING MARTYRDOM.

In our childhood the fate of martyrs burned at the stake or devoured by wild beasts seemed the most horrible that could be imagined. The experience of life throws a different light upon the subject. We have no less admiration for the noble devotion of those who sacrificed all things for their faith, but we see that the period of their greatest suffering was not in the final struggle, which was often a time of great triumph for them, but in the bitter trials which preceded it. The first agony of self-surrender, the fierce temptations that afterward assailed them, the loss of fortune, social position, relatives, friends, the cruel sneers of those who had never before spoken anything but words of kindness and affection—in these experiences was the real martyrdom, from which the flames of the fagot or the teeth and talons of the wild beasts were only a welcome deliverance. It is the martyrdom of living and not of dying that puts our faith to the severest test. A widowed mother who sees her only son drawn gradually and steadily into ways of sin till he is swallowed up in a vortex of dissipation; a wife whose husband, once so kind and loving, and so devoted to his little ones, yields to the power of strong drink till he is changed from a respected citizen to a drunken brute; parents who are obliged to witness the progress of a painful and lingering disease as it slowly but surely gains possession of the body of a beloved child—

these are mere suggestions of the countless forms of living martyrdom to which our common humanity is subject. The sum of it is beyond the grasp of the imagination. Much of the keenest suffering of human souls is unknown and unsuspected. The warm and loving heart of many a wife is a medium of slow torture to her from the coldness and indifference of her husband. Incompatibility of mind and temper is the source of untold misery in the world, not only between husbands and wives, but in families and among friends. It is needless to enlarge upon this topic. " Every heart knoweth its own bitterness," but—blessed thought!—God knows too. It is all a part of his wise plan for our discipline, sanctification, and preparation for the highest eternal joy—the joy of serving him. This does not mean that he planned and created those evils, but that, being inevitable conditions of our selfish and sinful state, he kindly takes possession of them, so to speak, and causes them to work together for the good of those who love him. Not one stroke of the chisel could be spared. It is right to pray, as Paul did, to be delivered from the trial, but if the only answer to our prayer is " My grace is sufficient for thee," we should accept the answer not only without murmuring, but with devout thankfulness, rejoicing in the infinite love that is willing to take so much pains to train us up for the everlasting kingdom. I know of one who had painted on the inside of his watch-case, opposite the dial, the words "All is well," so that every time he consulted his watch he was reminded of the truth that, whatever might be the experience of the moment, it would be turned into a blessing if he consecrated it to the loving Father whose care of us never ceases for a single instant.

God pities us in our trials, but he is too wise and loving

to be moved by sympathy to any abatement of the discipline we need. There is nothing so inexorable as love.

MARRIAGE.

Painful as the confession may be, there is no denying that a vast amount of unhappiness in the world springs directly or indirectly from marriage. "Who shall deliver me from the body of this death?" is a cry that is wrung from many hearts. Unfortunately, they too often fail to wait for deliverance, but proceed to free themselves by the unholy laws of divorce.

I do not propose to consider the extreme or "divorce" cases, but rather the laws of Divine Providence with relation to marriage in general.

Marriage was instituted and is providentially employed for three great ends.

1. The perpetuity of the race.
2. The union of two natures which are counterparts of each other. Swedenborg advances a theory or philosophy of marriage to this effect: Each human being is an expression of the being of God. Man represents his wisdom, and woman his love. Each is essential to the completeness of the other, and in heaven they are not regarded as two, but as one. It certainly seems that the continual use of the marriage relation in the Scriptures to illustrate the union of Christ and the church must have a deeper significance than is consistent with the prevailing ideas concerning that relation. It is the belief of many that in some way the union of two compatible natures is to be permanent. Charles Kingsley said: "I know not how it may be with others, but I know that I married my wife for all eternity." Writing to a friend on Luke xx. 35, "But they

which shall be accounted worthy to obtain that world, and the resurrection from the dead, neither marry, nor are given in marriage," he said: "If I do not love my wife, body and soul, as well there as I do here, then there is neither resurrection of my body nor of my soul, but of some other, and I shall not be I. Therefore, whatsoever the passage means, it cannot mean what the monks would make it." Space will not permit a more extended treatment of this topic.

3. The third purpose of marriage is the mutual helpfulness and discipline which belong to the condition. The first element does not exclude the second. If life is given us for discipline it is not to be expected that it will be left out of the most important and universal experience of life. Marriage inevitably brings discipline in many ways. However happily a husband and wife may be united, they necessarily bear somewhat the relation to each other that the diamond-dust of the lapidary bears to the diamond; they undergo a process of polishing by mutual attrition. The difference between the masculine and feminine temperaments, though essential to the very existence of the marriage relation, and the source or occasion of complete happiness in a perfect union, results in much unhappiness from the friction which naturally grows out of that difference while in our present imperfect, selfish state. A recognition of this truth is the only remedy. If each will accept the trials as a part of God's plan, strength will surely come to bear them. It must be constantly kept in mind that God makes no mistakes. He imposes no burdens for which strength will not be given. He foresaw all the distress that would come from the incompatibility you so deeply regret, and if you will accept it from his hand much

of the unhappiness will disappear, and for the remainder you may even have grace to be thankful, as a part of the plan for the building of your character and the shaping of your eternal destiny.

DURATION OF LIFE.

"It is *appointed* unto men once to die." So the Bible says, but who accepts that declaration in its full meaning? It is usually regarded as merely a statement of the fact that death is the common lot of all. But this is not the natural or most obvious signification of the word "appoint." By its etymology it indicates not only that all men are subject to death, but that the time and circumstance are fixed. In the revised version the translation "laid up for" is given in the margin. "It is laid up for all men to die." This is the only meaning that is consistent with the doctrine of Divine Providence. It seems a strange exercise of human judgment to believe that God directs and controls the events of our daily lives, and yet leaves the most important of all events—the termination of our lives—to the contingencies of disease or accident.

Faith in an Infinite Father's care leaves room for no such inconsistency. It believes that the time, the circumstances, everything that is connected with the death of each individual, is appointed, "laid up for" him. It may be by a lingering disease, with much suffering. It may be with a short and painful illness. It may be by the instantaneous stoppage of the heart's beating. It may be by accident. In any and all cases, life ends because God's time has come for it to end. For the wicked the moment has arrived when further probation would do more harm than good. For the righteous the discipline of life is to cease; his earthly education is completed. The work in the Father's kingdom for which he has been prepared is now ready for him.

A mistaken idea concerning the relation of the two worlds is a prominent cause of disbelief in the providential appointment of death for each and all. The general impression is that this world is for activity and labor, while heaven is for rest and repose. As labor and care are usually identical in this world, the freedom from care which we are promised in heaven is supposed to include or imply a cessation from all effort. When a good and useful man dies in the midst of life, we feel a degree of surprise that God should take him from the sphere of his active labor, as if we believed he was to be laid upon the shelf for all eternity. The more reasonable view of continuous life and continuous activity removes this misapprehension. God has as definite a work for us to do in the other world as in this. In some respects heaven is more of a field of work than earth, for this is not so much the time and place for definite labor as for preparation. Our work here is secondary to our discipline, and is an important part of it. There discipline will be at an end and labor will only be a joyful service, ever bringing its own reward.

The sufferings incident to sickness and death increase the difficulty of believing that it all must be included in God's plan. But we cannot reason upon the subject for a moment without realizing that if there is a Divine Providence it must include this experience equally with, if not above, all others. Our selfishness brought sin and death, but God, the Heavenly Father, promises in his infinite love to overrule these evils for the good of his children.

For those mourning the loss of relatives or friends who are dearer to them than life itself, nothing can be more sad than to doubt God's providence in the bereavement, and to suppose that the sickness or the accident was the result of a "general law" acting independently of our Father's care and purpose.

Dr. Hodge says: "If God is in the planet, he must be equally in the atom." Let us follow out this thought. There are floating in the atmosphere an inconceivable number of motes, particles, or molecules, many of them far too small to be discerned without the aid of a powerful microscope. They drift here and there, apparently guided by no law, subject to the caprice of every changing breeze. Can it be possible that each of those atoms is under the supervision of the Divine Providence, upheld by him and guided as truly by a purpose as the planet in its course? Undoubtedly. There is no escaping the conclusion. Science says the "potential force" is universal. The Bible says: "He causeth his wind to blow" and it is by the motion of the air that the unseen particles are distributed. "But these motes are so insignificant. It cannot be of the slightest consequence whether they move in one direction or the other." Is that true? Let us consider. Some of the particles are germs of a fatal disease. They enter the lungs of a beloved child. They remain for days or weeks, all unsuspected, yet constantly germinating and developing, till suddenly the form that seemed so full of life and health is smitten with the malignant fever, and through a dark valley of delirium and suffering the precious soul passes out into the Infinite Beyond. "Rachel mourns for her children, and will not be comforted because they are not."

Many of us have passed through this agonizing experience. Can we believe that those germs floating in the air were too small for our Father's notice and guidance? No; the heart that is oppressed by such a sorrow, if it has any faith, requires no process of logic to prove that the divine care embraced those unseen particles and used them as his servants. They were the messengers by which our loved ones were called to the heavenly home. "Death, under the Christian aspect, is but God's method of colonization, the transition from this mother-country of our race to the fairer and newer world of our emigration." "What we call life is a journey to death. What we call death is the gateway to life."

> There is no death; what seems so is transition;
> This life of mortal breath
> Is but a suburb of the life elysian,
> Whose portals we call death.

A premature death is not possible with God as the arbiter of our destinies. He alone can judge the heart and life. A gifted child is taken from our home, and we mourn the unfulfilled promise of so many useful qualities. But there was a spiritual maturity in that loving nature which we had not realized. The man of fourscore years who has not learned to love and do the will of God is not matured, while "the child shall die an hundred years old."

Watts's favorite lyric, "There is a land of pure delight," which has inspired and encouraged so many "timorous mortals," needs one emendation. The lines

> Death, like a narrow sea, divides
> That heavenly land from ours,

should read

> Death, like a narrow sea, unites
> That heavenly land to ours.

Death is a bond of union between the temporal and the eternal. If we were more susceptible to celestial influences we would find that even the present separation from our beloved ones is not as complete as we suppose. They now belong wholly to the "kingdom within," and as we cultivate that kingdom we shall have many sweet intimations of their presence.

> Say not of thy friend departed,
> He is dead; he has but grown
> Larger souled and deeper hearted,
> Blossoming into skies unknown:
> All the air of earth is sweeter
> For his being's full release;
> And thine own life is completer
> For his conquest and his peace.

CHAPTER X.

A RATIONAL HEAVEN.

In their anxiety to avoid the tendency of human nature to form a materialistic and sensuous conception of the future life, the religious teachers of the past have gone to the opposite extreme, and have filled our minds with an image of heaven which is neither possible nor desirable. From a literal interpretation of a restricted selection of texts they have given an impression of the heavenly life which is not consonant with the laws of our being. It is true that the crude ideas of the past are no longer accepted. No one now believes that the inhabitants of heaven will stand forever around a throne with harps in their hands, singing hymns of praise and casting their crowns at the feet of a sceptered Monarch. Yet, although such views are now generally discarded, no rational and consistent theory of the life beyond has been widely adopted in their place. A heaven of eternal idleness; a condition in which it is uncertain whether friends can recognize one another; a doubt as to the perpetuity of our present faculties and powers—these are a few of the indications that the popular idea is unnatural and impossible of realization, unless we are to be entirely re-created and changed into an order of beings whose characteristics and qualities shall be totally different from those we now possess.

Perhaps the question may be asked, Why not? Are we not distinctly told that "Eye hath not seen, nor ear heard, neither have entered into the heart of man the things which God hath prepared for them that love him"? Did not Paul say that he was caught up into paradise and heard unspeakable words which it is not lawful for a man to utter? Certainly; but a careful consideration of the subject will show that this does not prove what it has always been supposed to prove, namely, that the realities of heaven are essentially different from the realities of earth, and that they will not appeal to the faculties we now possess. If a native of Greenland should visit the tropics and see the magnificence of the vegetable world, the boundless varieties of animal life, the exquisite shapes and colors of the birds, and hear their songs, he would be compelled to use similar language in speaking to his countrymen of the marvelous things he had witnessed: "Eye hath not seen, nor ear heard, neither hath it entered into your Greenlandish hearts to conceive the wonders of that world." There are no objects in the polar regions to suggest to the untrained minds of such a people the commonest facts of the tropical world. Yet in Greenland may be found the same elements of life that are so much more fully and beautifully developed under tropical conditions.

How, then, can we gain a correct idea of the spiritual world, which must certainly vary from this material world more than Brazil differs from Greenland?

By a reasonable consideration of scriptural teachings, combined with an intelligent study of our own natures.

That our natures will remain essentially unchanged may almost be assumed as an axiom, notwithstanding the universal impression to the contrary. The Bible tells us that we are made in the image of God. The human type must therefore be the highest possible type. It is after the pattern of the infinite. Hence it cannot be altered without lowering it—a contingency which reason will not allow us to entertain for a moment. The difference between the conditions of this world and the spiritual world are suggested by the history of our own racial development. Who could have prophesied two hundred years ago what the occupations and pleasures of this age would be? They were almost as completely unknown and unsuspected as the ways of the heavenly world are to us now.

There is a conception of heaven which appeals so strongly to our highest reason that we feel its truth instinctively the moment it is presented. This conception or ideal regards heaven as a consummation of redeemed and perfected manhood; a place or condition in which our God-given faculties and powers, rescued from the thraldom of selfishness and sin, and consecrated to the service of our Maker, shall find eternal exercise. There is nothing more patent to our observation in this world than the purpose of the Power which rules over human destiny to secure the utmost variety of character among men, and to develop a distinct individuality in each member of the race. It is unreasonable to suppose that this process is carried on during the brief period of our temporary earthly life only to be reversed when the permanent life begins. "So careful of the type?" we may ask, in a somewhat different sense from the poet's meaning. So careful of the type in this world of shadows and then destroy it in the world of realities, bringing the myriads of the race down to one common pattern? It is not to be thought of.

The heavenly life is a life of service—divine service and

mutual service. The meaning of the word "angel" is "one sent." The inhabitants of heaven are angels or messengers because they are willing to be sent. Though distinct in their individuality, their will is one with God's. The purpose of our life here is to learn the lesson of self-surrender, of giving up our own selfish will and accepting the divine will in its stead. The entire paraphernalia of the material universe was created to this end. All our trials, all our afflictions, all experiences of every kind are sent or permitted as a part of God's plan for developing our characters and fitting each one of us for an eternal work—a work that no one else could do.

This conception is the only one that affords a consistent basis for the theory of a Divine Providence ruling our lives. Any attempt to explain that doctrine, or the scriptural statements concerning it, from the standpoint of this world alone, must fail. "A thousand shall fall at thy side, and ten thousand at thy right hand, but it shall not come nigh thee." Yet the pestilence *does* come to God's people, or to those whom they love more than their own life. It often appears that the most grievous afflictions are sent to those who are the most devoted to God's service. Such passages are meaningless unless we give them a purely spiritual interpretation. We are made to suffer through our bodies, our fortunes, our friends, through every possible avenue of outward circumstance. The promise is that the evils shall not come nigh *us;* that is, they will not be permitted to injure our eternal interests. On the contrary, they will be made to serve those interests if we will accept them in the right spirit.

The thought of heaven as a place of rest, though natural as a reaction from the discipline and weariness of life, has assumed an undue proportion, and has taken possession of our minds to the exclusion of more rational ideas. The common feeling is expressed in these lines:

> This life is all resistance and repression.
> Dear God, if in that other world unseen
> Not rest we find, but new life and progression,
> Grant us a respite in the grave between.

Charles Kingsley wrote, in the weariness of his exhausting labors: " When I get to heaven I think I would like to lie down with my head in my wife's lap and rest a thousand years." Such a feeling, though natural in this world, cannot be associated with our heavenly state. Rest is of value only as a relief from fatigue. Fatigue, at least of a painful and oppressive nature, belongs to our earthly condition, in which we are weighted down by the grossness of matter. The normal state of a human being is activity. The injunction of our Lord that we should become as little children has a broader meaning than we are wont to give it. The most marked characteristic of a child, next to its simplicity and trustfulness, is its intense love of activity. To plan, to act, to exercise its faculties in every possible way —this is the life and happiness of a child. When we become " as little children," and are in a world where love is the law of life, and all our conditions, influences, and impulses are normal, a life of activity and usefulness is the only existence that can be imagined as affording happiness. We do not need to inquire too closely with regard to the character and variety of our employments in the future life. The single declaration that we are to be ministering spirits opens a thousand avenues for useful and delightful service. Each individual possessing some quality or gift that no other has, each one thinking more of others' happiness than his own, each with a separate yet endlessly growing capacity for receiving love, truth, and wisdom from God, and giving out to others that which he receives—what more do we need to suggest an eternity of joy to a community of intelligent and loving beings?

Swedenborg says: "The life of the angels is the love of uses. Selfishness and death are with them synonymous. Their offices, employments, and duties, all for the good of others, are of infinite variety. Many of them are engaged in secret and constant services to the human race. There are angels of birth and death; angels who comfort in sickness and in sorrow; angels who instruct and enlighten; angels who defend from evil spirits; angels who lead the sweet thoughts of innocent children; angels who inspire conjugal love; and a thousand other genera and species of heavenly ministers."

And Spenser wrote of the angels:

> They for us fight, they watch and duly ward,
> And their bright squadrons round about us plant;
> And all for love, and nothing for reward.
> Oh, why should heavenly God to us have such regard?

If we as Christians condemn agnosticism, what right have we to assume the agnostic's position with reference to the heavenly world, and say that nothing can be known about it? Heaven is the world of realities, and earth is the world of shadows. The Rev. Dr. T. T. Munger says: "Science has led up to a point where matter and not God becomes the unknowable." Huxley says: "We know more of mind than we do of body. The immaterial world is a firmer reality than the material."

A rational study of the laws of our own being must therefore reveal to us something of the nature of the future life. The following description is so evidently reasonable that the mind instinctively accepts it rather as testimony than as theory, because it portrays a normal development of our own personal faculties:

> The human soul is of such a nature that there is no assignable limit to its capacities to know, love, and enjoy. . . . Every new accession of spiritual life enables us to bring forth more fruit. This is true of every created being. The faculties of the highest angels are continually enlarging and perfecting, and, consequently, they are bearing more abundant fruit, and of a more precious quality. This is true of every branch that beareth fruit. This truth holds out to us the glorious prospect that all our spiritual faculties in which there is any life will continue to enlarge and increase in excellence forever. We must, therefore, attain to a state of knowledge and wisdom compared with which the highest attainments of the greatest and most saintly men on earth are as the knowledge of an infant to the wisest sage. We must pass beyond all our conceptions of what is possible to the human mind. As we come nearer to the Lord the divine forces will operate more directly upon us; the divine attractions will become more powerful; we shall come more fully into the sphere of the divine influence, and into closer and more intimate communion with the Lord. Our faculties also will expand and we can receive larger measures of life. With every step of progress in knowledge there will be a corresponding increase in happiness. Desire and attainment, hope and fruition, will go hand in hand; consequently the final and constant effects of union with the Lord will be joy and peace. In all our glowing activities there will be no labor, in our highest aspirations no disappointment. As we come more fully into the sphere of the Divine Love and Wisdom, we shall come into a more perfect harmony, into a fuller joy, a sweeter peace, a deeper rest.[1]

A supposed distinction between angels and redeemed spirits in heaven has greatly misled us with reference to our occupations there. We read "He giveth his angels charge over thee," and similar passages, and have inferred that angels do the work while we are singing the praises

---

[1] Rev. Chauncey Giles.

of redeeming love. We are not warranted by the Scriptures as a whole in making such a distinction. In many of the biblical narratives, when angelic visitors are mentioned they are spoken of as men. The three angels who appeared to Abraham, the two who brought the warning to Lot, the angel who wrestled with Jacob, the one who appeared to Joshua at Jericho, are all called men. When John the revelator fell down to worship the angel who had shown him the wonders of the heavenly world, the angel said: " See thou do it not; for I am thy fellow-servant, and of thy brethren the prophets, and of them which keep the sayings of this Book."

In the Apocalypse we are told that the measurements of the holy city, the New Jerusalem, were "according to the measure of a man, that is, of the angel." All this is consistent with Paul's statement that we are to have bodies, and with innumerable allusions in the Bible to scenes in heaven which could only be enacted by beings with bodies similar to our own. They could not sit upon thrones without bodies, nor play upon a harp without hands, nor sing and talk without tongues, lips, and vocal organs, nor hear the music without ears, nor see the glories of the place without eyes.

Saint Augustine relates the following experience of a friend of his named Gennadius, who was a well-known physician at Carthage. He had a vision of a young man who conveyed him to a distant city and showed him many things there. Afterward the apparition appeared again and spoke with him. The young man said to Gennadius, "Where is your body now?" "In my bed." "Do you know that now you see nothing with the eyes of your body?" "I know it." "Well, then, with what eyes do you behold me?" As Gennadius hesitated, and knew not what to reply, the young man said to him: "In the same way that you see and hear me now that your eyes are shut and your senses asleep, thus after death you will live, see, and hear, but with eyes of the spirit."

> Space cannot mete
> The spiritual leagues that separate
> The soul from its primeval state:
> The race for peace is never to the fleet;
> Naught in this universe of sense is truly great.
>
> Nay, but another universe there is,
> Not visible, as this,
> Wider than space, though its immensity
> Between love-meeting lips may compassed be:
> Older than time,
> Yet glowing with immortal prime:
> Whose divine virility
> Breeds from each palpitating hour eternity;
> Within whose subtle bounds do dwell
> God's hosts of angels, and his wards in hell;
> O'er whose expanse no compass guidance lends,
> Yet which all those may traverse without chart
> Who own a human heart:
> Since 'tis the heart that journeys, and the journey lies
> Not elsewhere than within its principalities.[1]

Three elements should be taken into account in forming our views concerning the other life, viz., the sacred Scriptures, the nature of God, and the nature of man. From them we are led to the following conclusions:

1. Heaven is a spiritual world. It differs in its essence or quality from this world as the soul differs from the body. Hence its characteristics cannot be accurately judged by the standards of a material world.

2. But it is a *world*, and must therefore have the con-

[1] Julian Hawthorne.

stitution of a world; i.e., it must be made up of definite objects which have definite relations to one another.

3. As it is the soul and not the body which looks out upon the objects of the material world, and the soul and not the body which possesses the senses of sight, hearing, touch, taste, and smell, the inference is inevitable that objects in the spiritual world will appeal to those senses in some way corresponding to their uses in this world. In other words, the spiritual world is as much a world of realities to spiritual beings as the natural world is a world of realities to natural beings.

4 Cause and effect will have their relation and sequence in the spiritual world as in the natural world.

5. Hence the spiritual world is a world of growth or development.

The final postulate is the culmination of the other four, and a key to the Bible as a revelation of eternal truth.

The Christian church has suffered much in the past from the one-sidedness and the misleading emphasis of teachers. So much prominence has been given to the necessity for spiritual *birth* that the equal necessity for spiritual *growth* has been nearly lost sight of. In opposing the false doctrine of salvation by works, Protestantism has been carried to an opposite extreme in its advocacy of the dogma of salvation by faith alone. It would be equally logical and consistent to assert that our fate in this world depends upon "birth alone." In one sense it is true, for unless we are born we cannot have an earthly existence. Yet in reality the statement would be utterly false. From the moment of our birth the laws of growth must be obeyed, or we must perish. The Saviour's instructions invariably confirm and enforce this law of growth. He bids us consider the lilies of the field, how they *grow*. He is careful to explain it as a gradual process, "First the blade, then the ear; after that the full corn in the ear." It is like the mustard seed, the least of all seeds, which, when it is sown, becomes greater than all herbs. The graces he enjoins—humility, mercy, purity, and the others—are all such as can only become a part of our nature by a slow process of self-denial and self-abnegation.

Does the law of growth pertain only to our earthly condition? Do its operations cease at the moment of our leaving the body, "as if there were some magic in that little thing of dying"?[1] This may not be a positive teaching of theology, but it has been a scarcely avoidable inference from the doctrines as taught. We are made heirs of heaven by a single act of grace, and have only to wait for translation to the other side of the river of death to enter into the full possession of our rights. We must avoid sin because it is a Christian duty to do so, but the average instructions of the past have not made it clear that we are Christians only so far as we manifest the spirit of Christ, and that there is the same relation between our spiritual food and the growth of our souls that there is between our natural food and the growth of our bodies.[2]

Evolution, in its broadest meaning, is as truly a key to the spiritual world as to the physical. God is the author and source of all life. He is the only life. The living creatures he calls into being have no life in themselves, but are only varied recipients and manifestations of his life. For reasons of his own he has chosen to adopt the plan of introducing his life through a process of gradual develop-

---

[1] Phillips Brooks.
[2] This subject is treated more fully in the chapter on Spiritual Alchemy.

ment. Beginning with matter, which is now conceded to have a kind of life peculiar to itself, and passing from the lowest forms of vegetable existence through a continually rising scale to conscious or animal life, a point is finally reached when immortal life begins. The creature now partakes of the divine nature. *But the process remains unchanged.* By the adoption of a single word theology indorses the conclusions of science, and transfers God's methods from things material to things spiritual. In accepting the principle of *imparted* righteousness in place of the former dogma of *imputed* righteousness, the law of life in the physical universe is brought into the realm of spiritual laws, and the standard of the heavenly life is revealed. To be a Christian is to receive the life of God through Christ, and *that is a process which can never end.* God the giver is infinite. We the receivers are finite. Therefore in our development throughout eternity there can never be an end to his giving nor to our receiving. In the light of this truth all things fall into perfect order and harmony. A key is afforded to the mysterious problems of life, the ways of God to man in the methods of Divine Providence are justified, and in place of an impossible heaven we have a conception which serves as a perpetual inspiration to those who accept it.

Yet there is an important corollary to this truth. If the doctrine of a magical transformation at death is discarded, some kind of an intermediate process is rendered necessary. There can be no question that, as has been said, " we leave this world in all stages of an uncompleted development." A conviction has been felt by many minds that an intermediate state is a logical necessity. The Scriptures contain various allusions to a middle state which is called "sheol." Jacob said, "I shall descend unto my son in sheol mourning." It is generally agreed by biblical scholars that sheol is the place of disembodied souls. Beecher said, a short time before his death: "I believe there is an intermediate state, although I cannot give satisfactory proof or authority for the belief." Dr. Charles A. Briggs says: "The progress in sanctification goes on after death." He also says: "Immediate sanctification at death is an error added on to the orthodox doctrine of sanctification that makes it inconsistent, and virtually destroys it." He has in the same paragraph already described sanctification as " a work that is carried on by God in a gradual process."

The doctrine of immediate sanctification and the theory of an angelic transformation at death appeal almost irresistibly to the selfish or the indolent side of human nature. It is so comfortable to have the work done for us with only the necessity for our accepting it ready-made. This fallacy is trenchantly exposed by Professor Drummond in his chapters on parasitism and semi-parasitism in "Natural Law in the Spiritual World." The error is doomed, but it falls in too easily with our natural spirit of indolence and self-indulgence to die without a struggle.

The inconsistency of the "immediate" theory is sharply revealed when we try to account for the differences of character and condition that must exist in heaven. No one is willing to argue for universal uniformity among redeemed spirits, but all are puzzled (on the old theory) to account for the distinction which it is felt must exist. Here is a noble, self-sacrificing Christian who has been tried in God's seven-heated furnace, and the very spirit of his Master stands revealed in his character and deeds. Here is another, who seems to be a sincere disciple of Christ, yet how imperfect is his nature! How much that is petty and unlovely still remains to be overcome! They both pass over to the other side. Are they to receive a similar reward? "Oh no," it is said. "One star differeth from another in glory. The first has a far greater capacity for happiness than the second. The cup of each will be full, but one cup will be much larger than the other." Let the reader of these pages ask himself if that method of reasoning has ever really satisfied him. He has accepted it because he saw no alternative, but never, I think, without an inward protest.

In contrast with that mechanical doctrine, how dignified, consistent, and satisfying is the law of spiritual growth, with Christ, the Divine Lord, as the author of our life. "I am the vine, ye are the branches. He that abideth in me and I in him, the same bringeth forth much fruit." What right have we to limit such declarations to this transitory world? All the laws of reason and analogy are against such limitation.

The necessity for an intermediate state grows out of the restricted and artificial conditions of our life in the flesh. We cannot see the soul of our dearest friend; we only see a mask. Human features and human language can, with the best intentions, but very imperfectly reveal the inmost thought and life. More than this, we are ignorant even of our own real motives. We may be confident that, on the whole, we love good better than evil, and desire to be children of the Heavenly Father. But it is impossible to know how far the secret springs of our life may still be under the dominion of selfishness. While subject to that control, we surely are not fully ripe for heaven.

The soul in the intermediate state has been compared to seed planted in the soil. The possibilities were all there before, but the seed is now placed in a condition which admits the evolution of its latent capacities. The hidden germ unfolds and develops in accordance with the law of its being. So the spirit, released from the hindering medium of the flesh and the complex influences of its earthly environment, has an opportunity to follow freely its own impulses, to act out its own nature. No one while in the body is entirely free from wrong inclinations and hurtful tendencies. Doubtless there are many consecrated souls whose tarrying in the intermediate condition is but short, and many others with whom the love of evil is so predominant that they gravitate to "their own place" with but little delay. The average Christian, however, seems to be in a state which requires no little of the winnowing process.

It may be said that this theory is discouraging. Is the struggle of life, after all, to be carried with us into the beyond? Are we only to repeat there on a larger scale the disheartening experiences of this mortal existence?

No; the conditions will be totally changed. We will not there be "cribbed, cabined, and confined" as we are in the earthly state. We are here under restrictions of the flesh, of society, of civil law. No one acts out perfectly his own nature. He could not if he would and he would not if he could. While the body is the expression of the soul, it is also a perpetual hindrance to the free exercise of its powers.

But in the spiritual world, according to all the suggestions of the Scriptures, the laws of analogy, and the prophetic instincts of our own being, restrictions of every kind will be removed. If we love our Lord and desire to follow him, the outgoings of our hearts will be spontaneous and free. No weaknesses of the flesh will hinder us, evil associations will be withdrawn from us, every pure and holy impulse will have a natural expression and growth; and in proportion as we are prepared for it we shall rise toward that " third heaven " where Paul's unutterable things were seen.

What a new incentive does this view of the truth afford to the struggling Christian! Who is not willing to deny himself every earthly indulgence when he feels that by thus doing he is developing and enlarging his being for the other life, and lifting himself up toward celestial heights? What a divine miracle it is that by a faithful and loving performance of our humblest duties here we are promoting our angelic growth, and enlarging our capacity to receive and enjoy the infinite love of God.

Can we turn our thoughts from this glorious vision to the dark side of the picture? If we are there to be left free to follow good, we shall be equally free to give ourselves up to the opposite. How sad to think of those who will eagerly turn toward evil because they have learned to love it! Yet there is a truth that is sadder still. Our Saviour taught us, in language as solemn and impressive as he could make it, that some of us who regard ourselves as his followers, who " in his name have done many wonderful works," will find that the underlying principle of our life was selfishness, and therefore we can have no part or lot with him. Bunyan closes his immortal allegory with these words: " Then I saw that there is a way to hell even from the gates of heaven as well as from the City of Destruction."

CHAPTER XI.

THE GREAT INSANITY—LIVING FOR THIS WORLD.

A LITTLE child is the ideal of all that is beautiful. There is no object on earth so lovely, so attractive. We watch its play with unceasing interest and pleasure. The home is its world. The doll and the hobby-horse are endowed by its imagination with all the qualities of life.

Now let us suppose a group of children to continue the same infantile life and methods as they grow older. How soon the charm would be gone! The ways which were once so charming would become repellant, distressing, and finally unbearable. If they should continue thus unto the period of manhood and womanhood we would be compelled to pronounce them hopelessly insane. They could not be called idiotic, for idiots do not exhibit the intelligence of little children.

Insanity. No milder term will characterize such a condition as has been described. Yet are not the lives of vast numbers of the human race analogous to this? They do not amuse themselves with children's toys, it is true, but are their minds any more worthily occupied because their amusements happen to be of a different character? I do not refer merely to the so-called pleasures of the world. I include all the ambitions of life—anything and everything that is done solely with reference to this world. Even literature which does not have a moral purpose is simply a kind of toy.

This devotion to earth-centered occupations I call *The Great Insanity*. A youth would be pronounced insane who deliberately gave himself up for one week to a course of pleasure or self-gratification which he knew would bring ruin and disgrace upon the remaining fifty years of his life. In what respect do we show any greater sanity by using our fifty or seventy years without regard to the eternity that is to follow? However wide the disparity between the week and the years, that between the span of life and eternity is infinitely wider. Be the years ever so tedious and seemingly interminable, there is one thing certain: they will surely and inevitably end, while the ages of eternity are no nearer a termination after a thousand million years have passed than they are to-day.

It is no fault of the Bible if men allow themselves to be deluded into the idea that this life has any element of permanency or any value in itself. How striking is the language whenever this subject is presented! What is life? It is like grass, which is fresh and beautiful in the morning, but is cut down and withers in an hour. It is like a mist, which appeareth for a little time and then vanisheth away. In Job it is compared to a sail on the horizon that glistens before our sight for a moment and then disappears. No language can be conceived to give a more striking impression of that which is evanescent and fleeting than the terms employed in the Scriptures to describe our earthly condition. Yet, with the fatuity of blind human nature, we treat such descriptions as merely poetical. "What beautiful and effective illustrations!" we say, and lose all the force of the lesson in our admiration of the language by which it is conveyed. Certainly, it is poetry of the highest order, but it is God's poetry, which is equivalent to saying that it is also the truth. He never sacrifices the real for the ideal. His real is ideal. That human life is like a passing cloud or a transient flower is the exact, mathematical truth. Professor Drummond says: "The world is only a thing that is. It *is* not. It is a thing that teaches, yet not even a thing—a show that shows, a teaching shadow."

It does not seem so to us. The "cosmic dust" in which our being is inclosed proves a wonderfully effective medium for excluding us from a consciousness of the realities of spiritual things. That was the divine purpose, and, like all of God's plans, it is thoroughly accomplished. Our delusion on this point is so complete that we are disposed to regard our decaying bodies as real and substantial, while the never-dying spirit within is thought of as unsubstantial and unreal.

The change of conception from one point of view to the other is truly a change from a condition of insanity to one of rationality. What is insanity? It is unsoundness of mind. It is a derangement of the thoughts. An insane person puts a few feathers in his hair and thinks he wears a crown. He hoards a handful of pebbles in a corner and is rich with uncounted gold. Truly he would be right if all men agreed with him. If all were under the same delusion, the world would be full of crowns and gold.

A false idea of values is an indication of insanity. He who reckons pebbles as gold, and builds his plans of life upon that estimate, must expect to be regarded as a madman, and if he tries to force his views upon others he must expect to be treated as such.

Where can we find a more ruinous misinterpretation of values than in the case of those who live in Christian communities, who have read or heard the Bible all their lives, and therefore know what the true standard is, and who yet go through the world treating pebbles as gold and gold as pebbles. The merchant who overreaches his neighbor in a business transaction, the lawyer who perverts justice by unworthy tricks, the minister of the blessed gospel who preaches only for fame, the farmer who is not moved to gratitude to God by the miracle of creation which gives him his yearly harvest—these and all others of whom they are types are reckoning pebbles as gold; they are bartering eternal joys for a little *seeming* good in the few days of this feverish existence.

One of the elements of this earthly insanity is a misconception of the duration of life. The testimony of God's Word carries no weight against the evidence of our senses. "Life *seems* long, therefore it *is* long," is the form of logic with which we delude ourselves. It has been said by survivors of vessels which have foundered at sea, that when the fatal blow was struck, and the moment arrived when it was found that all hope was lost, a great cry or shriek went up from the awe-struck company of human beings who were so soon to leave the world. This frantic expression of their feelings has usually been attributed to a sudden awaking of remorse. I do not think so. It seems rather to arise from the sudden dispelling of life's illusions. Every person in that shuddering crowd who had been living for this world, with the idea that the objects of his pursuits were *realities* worthy of his time and attention, was brought to see, in an instant, the fatal error.

One evidence of universal hallucination is to be observed in the misuse or misapplication of the word "ruin." Our plans fail of success, or we are unfortunate in a business enterprise, and we straightway cry out that we are "ruined." If the worst happens that we anticipate, what is the ruin which excites our terror? That we are obliged to move from a large house into a smaller one, to wear plainer clothing and eat plainer food, to be a clerk, perhaps, instead of a proprietor, or, at the worst, to earn our daily bread by painful labor. There is no denying that such a change is a trial and a hardship. But it is the farthest possible from "ruin." It is much more likely to prove salvation by removing a thousand temptations from our pathway. The ruined people are those whom God leaves undisturbed in their luxurious and self-indulgent lives, because, knowing the heart of every man, he sees that they would not be softened, but hardened, by the loss of their possessions.

A reeling drunkard is universally recognized as a ruined man. But we are apt to forget that the Bible, while it condemns drunkenness, yet has far more to say about the sin of covetousness. The covetous man who walks the streets with a proud consciousness of his wealth and the power it gives, has no idea of the leprous state of his soul in God's sight. Christ freely forgave the outcast and the fallen, but had only words of indignant scorn and condemnation for the proud Pharisees. Why? Was it because he does, after all, make a difference between men, and love some more than others? No. His ways are equal. He changes not. The Pharisees had converted God's blessed gifts into mere servants for their own self-indulgence, leading them to a feeling of contempt for their fellow-men. They were satisfied with themselves, and even infinite love could do nothing for them. They could only be used as danger-signals to warn the world of one of the broad avenues to perdition—the steep down-grade of unconsecrated prosperity.

How can the children of men be roused from their spiritual stupor? How can they be saved from the insane delusion which leads them to center their plans, their thoughts, their hopes, upon this ephemeral existence? Some of the agencies which are employed by our Heavenly Father for this purpose will be considered in the following chapter.

CHAPTER XII.

OUR SCHOOLMASTERS—UNCERTAINTY, SUFFERING, DEATH, CATASTROPHE, NATURE.

THERE are many who say that God cannot be good and permit such a vast amount and such infinite varieties of wretchedness and misery as are to be seen in the world. If we accept immortality as a factor in the problem, it immediately becomes apparent that the unhappiness of humanity, instead of indicating a want of beneficence in the Supreme Being, affords the strongest possible evidence of his infinite wisdom and goodness.

Let us consider the plan in its full scope and bearing. In order to create a race of beings possessing genuine character, with individuality, and a capacity for receiving and enjoying the divine life, it was necessary to place them in some kind of closed conditions in which they would be unconscious of any restraining influence, and could thus act, choose, and live in entire independence. This separation from the unseen, to accomplish its work must be so complete that they would have no consciousness of a life other than their own. Would it be kind, wise, or just to place them in such a condition without supplying some counteracting influence? Could any more beneficent plan be imagined than that their wanderings should inevitably bring suffering, and that their suffering should be in proportion to the distance they placed between themselves and the source of their life and happiness?

The human race was thus placed and has thus wandered. They are so far in their consciousness from the world to which they properly belong that they scarcely believe in its existence. What infinite cruelty it would be for their Creator to now leave them to their delusions, and take no measures to heal them of the insanity into which they have fallen. Such neglect would be contrary to the divine law of love. As we study God's dealings, we see that nothing could be more perfectly adapted to arouse attention and to win our thoughts and affections away from this world than the trying experiences that he sends or permits to come into our lives. These are of such a disciplinary nature that they may be spoken of as our schoolmasters. They may be divided into four general classes, namely, Uncertainty, Suffering, Death, Catastrophe. We will consider them in the above order.

UNCERTAINTY.

Nothing in this world is permitted to be fixed and settled. Although the promise was given, " While the earth remaineth, seed-time and harvest, and cold and heat, and summer and winter, and day and night shall not cease," yet in their relation to each individual there is a perpetual element of uncertainty. This is indicated by another passage from Holy Writ: " In the morning sow thy seed, and in the evening withhold not thine hand: for thou knowest not whether shall prosper, either this or that, or whether they both shall be alike good." The best and most useful works of man are usually produced with painful doubt and perplexity. The inventor works for years in giving a practical form to some great idea without the satisfaction of knowing whether his efforts will finally meet with success or failure. The author writes a book with mingled hope and fear, but cannot tell whether his thoughts will find a place in the world or sink into immediate oblivion. What could have a greater tendency to loosen the grasp of our affections upon this life than such a perpetual and harassing uncertainty? Yet so strongly do earthly influences appeal to us that the lessons of this teacher would exercise very little influence upon us if they were not supplemented by a monitor to whose voice we must perforce listen whether we will or not. This stern monitor is

SUFFERING.

In this title is included all forms of distress, whether physical, mental, or moral. Physical pain at least arrests our attention. If long continued, the point comes at last when we are compelled to cry out, "Why is this agony sent upon me? Why can I have no relief?" Thus the process of questioning is begun. Happy are we if our questioning leads to the only true answer—" Our Heavenly Father in his wise providence is permitting this suffering in order to show us our weakness and dependence, and to lead us to call upon him for help. He does not send it in anger, but in love. He is willing to inflict pain for a little while that we may learn patience and submission, and thus be prepared for the better things of the everlasting life."

Of mental and moral suffering there are forms without number. The solicitude of parents with regard to the welfare of their children enters with severe discipline into many lives. The anxieties of business men are a common source of mental suffering. It is impossible even to suggest the numberless forms of inward distress that the children of men are subject to. Very many of them are secret sorrows, unknown and unsuspected even by our nearest friends. This gives an added weight to the burdens. They finally become so great that we are forced to fly to the one final Source of comfort, consolation, and strength. This is just what our loving Father meant from the beginning. He does not willingly afflict or grieve us, but he loves us too much to leave us contented with our separation from him. So he sends these faithful messengers, Pain and Suffering, because nothing less severe will draw our thoughts from the charms and fascinations of the world, and dispel its vain illusions. It would seem that two such schoolmasters as the uncertainty of all human plans and the universality of pain and suffering ought to dispel our hallucinations and lead us to consider the true end of life. But the spell under which we live is too potent. In addition to the natural delusions of the flesh, Satan and his emissaries are ever at hand to spread an artificial glamour before our vision and persuade us that the earthly life is worth living in spite of all its drawbacks and disadvantages. One falsehood they never cease to repeat, nor we to believe—that our troubles will soon come to an end; that happiness lies just before us. Only one more corner will have to be turned, and the rough and difficult path will be exchanged for a broad highway of earthly prosperity and pleasure. It is evident, therefore, that a still more stern and uncompromising teacher is needed to impress upon us the deep meaning of life. Such a schoolmaster we have, and his name is

DEATH.

His instructions not only give us a new lesson, but they include the severity of the two teachers already described. All earthly things must vanish in a moment. When? Here we have the element of uncertainty in its most trying form. Moreover, when the time arrives it brings with it a great burden of pain, physical or mental, or both, for ourselves and our friends. It should not be so. Our sins and self-will have turned what ought to be a natural transition and a happy translation to a higher condition of life into a dark and painful ordeal. As such, its discipline is of the severest kind. Even the **Christian**, who looks forward to it with pleasure, and desires, with **Paul**, " to depart and be with Christ," still suffers keenly in the loss of kindred and friends. To the people of the world death is a dark enemy, a direful calamity, an evil thought, to be banished from their minds by every device that ingenuity can invent. Yet still it comes with inevitable tread. It smites a child, a husband, a wife, a brother, the dearest friend we have. How can its lessons pass unheeded? Surely we can never again return to our old follies or become interested as we were before in our earthly pursuits. Yet how soon the impressions fade away! The tide of worldliness rolls in and the lesson is forgotten. Who can deny the insanity of such a state? It would seem that the last resource of our Father was exhausted in his efforts to save humanity from its fatal delusions. If the absolute certainty of death and the absolute uncertainty of its hour cannot arrest the attention of intelligent human beings, what can possibly be added to increase the emphasis of the lesson? Just one resource is left, and if there is one, we may be certain that Infinite Wisdom will not fail to employ it. This fourth and final teacher may be described by the word

CATASTROPHE.

As the sickness, pains, and death of individuals leave many hearts still untouched, the smiting of numbers at the same time is occasionally permitted to deepen the tragedy of life, and teach lessons that other and less striking forms of calamity have failed to convey. A terrible accident, a fire, a flood, a pestilence—by such means a community, and, through the telegraph, the entire world, is startled out of its pleasure-seeking and its indifference to higher claims. It would be commonplace to enlarge upon this theme. Every reader can follow out his own thoughts and gain more profit than by any amplification of the topic by another. That great calamities are intended to teach important lessons is so obvious a truth that none will desire to question it except those who deny the existence of a Supreme Being. There are other sides of the subject which are treated in the chapter on Some Dark Problems.

The teachers thus far spoken of have been the stern and severe ones; those who come to us with a frown; who teach us their lessons by sore discipline and painful scourgings. Let us not make the sad mistake of supposing that they indicate in the most remote degree God's disposition toward us. If they seem to have a predominant part in his dealings with us, it is only because we make it necessary. The wilful child finds his school a place of trial because his many misdemeanors bring him in conflict with all its rules, and thus make him subject to its various forms of punishment. So it is with us in the school of life. In reality our Heavenly Father's kind and loving methods of instruction outnumber the severe ones a thousandfold. They will now be considered under the title of

NATURE.

Nature is one vast object-lesson, to teach us of God and spiritual things. "Earth is a parable of heaven." "Day unto day uttereth speech, and night unto night showeth knowledge." The sun arises in the morning with its flood of light, which reveals all earthly objects, and at the same time serves as a curtain to shut out the great universe beyond. It hides the stars and secludes our planet to itself. Then all things "utter speech." Every sight and every sound conveys a lesson. After a few hours the sun departs, the resplendent curtain is withdrawn, and the deeper revelations begin. The earth is seen

> . . . though in itself
> Complete and perfect all, yet but a part
> And atom of the living universe.

Night unto night showeth knowledge by uncovering the awful mysteries of the stars and permitting us to gaze into the depths of the infinite.

The spiritual lessons of the physical universe could not be understood or even imagined till science arose to show us the methods of an immanent God. An instantaneous world, called into being by the fiat of an external deity, could only remotely and imperfectly reveal his character. A world of growth, created and sustained by the living presence of God in its minutest parts, is a direct and perpetual revelation of the Divine Mind.

A snow-flake falls upon our sleeve. We observe it carefully. It is a perfect geometrical figure. Another falls. It is a different shape, as perfect in its outlines and even more beautiful than the first. Whence comes this marvelous law of crystallization? "The principle is inherent in nature," says the materialist. How irrational is such a theory if no intelligent First Cause is acknowledged as the source of this inherent principle! It has been aptly said that the materialists are polytheists inasmuch as they worship the countless millions of original atoms. The little child or the ignorant peasant who thinks that God makes the snow-flakes and sends them down upon the world holds a far deeper philosophy than the man of science, who can talk wisely about the law of crystallization, but denies the divine source of the law, or " does not know " its origin.

The universe is now more than ever an object-lesson in spiritual things because its laws are beginning to be recognized as spiritual. As the earth, a material body, is held together by attraction, it has heretofore been supposed that attraction is some kind of a material force. This fallacy is rapidly passing away. Attraction is not a material force. It is Will, and Will is another name for God. " He alone hath life in himself."

Philo Judæus, writing about the time of Christ, asserted that the derivation of the physical world from the spiritual world is expressly taught in the Book of Genesis. "These are the generations of the heavens and of the earth, . . . and of every plant of the field *before it was in the earth*, and of every herb of the field *before it grew*," which words, says Philo, " do manifestly teach that before the grass was green verdure already existed, that before the grass sprang in the field there was grass, though it was not visible.

The same must we understand from Moses in the case of everything else which is perceived by the external senses; there were older forms and motions already existing, according to which the others were fashioned and measured out. The things which he mentioned are examples of the nature of all."

All things in this world, therefore, speak to us of the spiritual nature within us. There are even fierce beasts and venomous reptiles to show what our godlike faculties may resemble if we turn away from the Source of goodness and yield our powers to the devil of selfishness. Upon this side of the picture we do not need to dwell.

Every object of beauty that strikes the eye, every sweet voice of nature that falls upon the ear, tells of an eternal reality that lies behind it. And every charm, whatever other suggestion it offers, conveys the one perpetual and much-needed lesson of the transient, evanescent character of all earthly experiences. The bird sings a sweet song and vanishes. We gather a lovely flower and it withers in our hand. Perhaps we have wealth, and think we can store up the beautiful things of nature. We build a conservatory and fill it with the choicest results of floriculture. But even our senses are palled. The eye becomes weary with seeing, and the exquisite fragrance ceases to act upon the nerves.

Sitting at my window one morning at the beginning of June, when Nature was at the height of her verdant loveliness, a yellow leaf came fluttering down from a neighboring tree with an untimely suggestion of decay. The meaning of the scene suddenly flashed upon my mind. What I was looking upon was not a reality; it was only a lesson. The entire world is only "a thing that teaches;

yet not even a thing—a show that shows, a teaching shadow." God sends the springtime and the flowers to suggest to us the beauties of our heavenly home, and then begins at once to remove them, as if he said: "Do not imagine these to be realities. They are only imperfect specimens of what you are to enjoy when you have graduated from the school of life, and are called to your Father's mansions to walk by the beautiful river and to wander in the celestial gardens."

> There *everlasting* spring abides,
> And *never-withering* flowers.

"Here we have but a few detached sketches of the panorama which belongs *there*, and what few we have, albeit they are so lovely, we see but 'as through a glass, darkly.' It will not be so always. The spiritual world known to philosophy is no other than the spiritual world of the hopeful Christian—the very same which we shall consciously inhabit when by death we cease to be conscious of the present. Our introduction in this life to mineral, vegetable, and animal, to air and sky and sun, is the beginning of a friendship that will never be dissolved, only that hereafter we shall view things as they really are, instead of their effigies and pictures. In this world we do not so much live as *prepare* to live, nor enjoy nature's sweet amenities as *prepare* to enjoy them. We shall leave it, but we shall not lose its beauty; we shall learn rather how most thoroughly to delight in it, often turning in pleased remembrance to those early days which now we reckon as our lifetime, and to that little sphere which was our birthplace and education."[1]

---

[1] Leo. H. Grindon, in "Life, its Nature, Varieties, and Phenomena."

CHAPTER XIII.

OUR COURSE OF STUDY.

IN the school of life the studies are not elective. At college we may decide whether classical, mathematical, or scientific subjects shall occupy the larger share of our attention. But in this terrestrial academy there is no such choice. Its curriculum embraces love, obedience, self-sacrifice, truthfulness, and purity. The alternative of not mastering those studies is the being mastered by their opposites. The new view of heaven as a consummation of earthly experience, a continuation of the evolutionary process under changed conditions, introduces into the problem of human education a fresh and hitherto unemployed set of factors and influences. It is, indeed, the beginning of a distinctly new process in the training of the race. Hitherto the educational method has had small place in the religious scheme. The doctrine of "imputed righteousness" leaves little room for it. As the result of our faith the character of Christ is miraculously imputed or transferred to us. It requires effort to live his life and resist temptation while in this world, but at death the soul goes to heaven, where the imputed righteousness of the Saviour will be received in full, and temptations and struggles are done with forever. This is the "gospel scheme," which grew out of the governmental or monarchical theory of God's relation to mankind. It was all the world was ready for, and it has done a glorious work. But this does not prove that the system itself was correct.

Evolution necessitates a radical change in the methods of spiritual instruction by revealing the world as a school, and life as a process of education. Yet this in reality only leads us back to the methods of Christ and the apostles. Jesus was not only the Great Exponent of the law of self-sacrifice, he was also the Great Teacher. In simple language and with plain and homely illustrations he continually enforced the lessons of a self-denying life. The Epistles, also, are almost wholly occupied with instruction. It was only by choosing individual texts and passages here and there that the scholastics were able to build up their systems. That the Epistles have been made to uphold every system which men have devised is conclusive evidence that the authors of the systems did not possess the true key or governing principle. The apostles only strove to present in every possible form the love of God for mankind as expressed in the life and work of the Lord Jesus Christ.

It is worse than useless, it is suicidal, to ignore the changed aspect of Protestant views in this new age. Dr. C. A. Briggs presents the case as follows in his book entitled "Whither?":

"Religion in Great Britain and America is at present in a very unsatisfactory condition. There is a wide-spread dissatisfaction with the old theology, and the old methods of worship and church work. At the same time there is distrust and anxiety with reference to new theology and new measures that are proposed by recent theological doctors. The ministers do not care to preach to empty pews, and besides, not a few of the ministers sympathize with their people in these matters. The ministers are in a feverish condition. Some are desirous of adapting the old theology and old methods to the new conditions and circumstances; others are opposed to any changes in the old types; there are some hot champions of the new, and there are some sturdy defenders of the old; but the majority do not care to disturb the peace, and are waiting for light and guidance."

Light and guidance have come, and we have only to make use of them. The theory of an indwelling God, expressing himself in nature, and striving to express himself in every individual of the human race, affords an unlimited source of instruction and inspiration. This is a theme which we, the occupants of church pews, will never weary of hearing discussed. We wish to hear of a God who is interested in the smallest affairs of every life; of a Heavenly Father who is every instant and by every possible means striving to draw all his erring children to himself; who, after they have turned toward him, still continues with untiring love to use every human experience, every incident, accident, influence, as a means of uniting them to him more intimately, with the growth of soul-character and the increase of happiness which invariably accompany that union. We wish to hear of a God who is with the righteous capitalist as he plans, with the justice-loving merchant as he buys and sells, the farmer as he sows and reaps, the housekeeper in her cares, the servant in the kitchen, the teacher with her handful of rustic children in the corner school-house, the invalid on a bed of pain, the physician who attends him; in brief, with every human being in every possible phase of human experience. We wish to hear of a God who is thus with all men not because he is a mighty monarch who can graciously condescend to visit his people out of a complaisant good-will, but who presses himself upon them because it is his nature so to do, because he created them expressly that he might give himself to them, and is infinitely pained and grieved when they refuse to accept him.

This is not a new gospel. It is the gospel of the Old Testament when spiritually understood. It is the gospel of the Lord Jesus Christ, freed from accretions of eminent writers of the past. It is a wonderful, divine fact that the teachings of Jesus (and also of the apostles when viewed in the light of his truths) are perfectly adapted to the laws of evolution. As the biblical account of creation gave the outlines of the process which was to be revealed by astronomy and geology thousands of years after it was written, so do the words of Christ embody the laws of spiritual growth which belong to the evolutionary method.

The world was not ready for the simple truth when our Lord came upon his mission. At the beginning of the Christian era mankind was emerging from the physical stage. The arts were cultivated to some extent, and literature began to be felt as a power in the world. But the moral element in man's nature was still undeveloped; it was scarcely regarded with any respect. The order of development is, first the physical being, next the intellectual, and finally the moral and spiritual. First the body, then the brain, and lastly the heart. The brain period of human history was then dawning, and the experiences which belong to that stage and condition were inevitable. The teachings of Christ, dealing only with plain and fundamental truths, did not afford aliment for the intellectual and metaphysical demands of the first eighteen centuries after the advent, but the needs of the age were fully met by the more polemical writings of the apostles. That they appeared as they did and served that necessary purpose is one of the most striking providences to be observed in the entire history of the race.

The preparatory course is now nearly ended. The world may be said to be entering its senior year in God's great university. Its studies have already been mentioned. Their method of treatment will be considered in the succeeding chapter. Although a mastery of all the branches is required, yet no student need fail to graduate, for the Great Teacher who furnishes the instruction also supplies the capacity to receive and apply it.

CHAPTER XIV.

SPIRITUAL ALCHEMY, OR THE LAW OF GROWTH.

How can the dross of our human nature be changed to pure gold? By what process of spiritual chemistry can we earth-born creatures be made ready for companionship with the divine?

Our Saviour said it was to be accomplished by our becoming joined to him as the branch is joined to the vine; by eating his flesh and drinking his blood. His language on this point is truly extraordinary. He repeats and reiterates the statement as if he wished it to be understood as containing the very essence and marrow of his gospel.

"*I am the living bread which came down from heaven: if any man eat of this bread, he shall live forever: and the bread that I will give is my flesh, which I will give for the life of the world. . . .*

"*Verily, verily, I say unto you, Except ye eat the flesh of the Son of man, and drink his blood, ye have no life in you.*

"*Whoso eateth my flesh, and drinketh my blood, hath eternal life; and I will raise him up at the last day.*

"*For my flesh is meat indeed, and my blood is drink indeed.*

"*He that eateth my flesh, and drinketh my blood, dwelleth in me, and I in him.*

"*As the living Father hath sent me, and I live by the Father; so he that eateth me, even he shall live by me.*

"This is that bread which came down from heaven: not as your fathers did eat manna, and are dead: he that eateth of this bread shall live forever."

The interpretation given to these most remarkable words has been sometimes used to support a doctrinal system. They have been applied to the sacrificial death of Christ as an atonement for the sins of mankind, and to satisfy the divine justice. But Jesus Christ did not come into the world to satisfy the divine justice; he came to reveal the divine love.

He himself has given us a clue to his meaning in the statement: "As the living Father hath sent me, and I live by the Father; so he that eateth me, even he shall live by me." How did he live by the Father? Clearly and only by doing his will. He came not to destroy the law, but to fulfil it. He fulfilled the law not to obviate the necessity of our fulfilling it, but that the way might be prepared for us to fulfil it. He overcame our spiritual enemies, he conquered death and hell that we might follow him and gain the victory in his name and by his strength.

The instructions of the apostles are consistent with this truth if they are taken naturally and not artificially. If the Epistles are read in the light of the Saviour's teachings, and not with a view to supporting a certain theory, system, or "plan of salvation," they will be found in beautiful accord with the laws of spiritual growth. Take the statement of Paul, which has been a bone of contention for so many centuries, "The just shall live by faith." A purely theological meaning has been given to it, as if Paul said, "The just shall *be born* by faith."

Taking the words naturally, and free from all preconceived ideas, what meaning do they convey? The revised version renders it: "The righteous shall live by faith." That is, those who are trying to do right have a certain source of life. What is it? It is faith. Paul has just said in the preceding verse that the gospel of Christ is the power of God unto salvation to every one that believeth. Unfortunately the word "believe" has also come to be taken in a technical and limited sense, as if it referred only to that act of receiving or believing in Christ which constitutes the new birth. There is no ground whatever for such a limitation. If we will, throughout the Epistles, substitute the word "uprightness" (of life) for "righteousness" (a theological term), and the word "receive" for "believe," we shall avoid nearly all the difficulties that have grown out of the theological controversies of the past. We are to receive the life of Christ as a plant receives the light and heat of the sun, or as the branch receives the life-blood of the vine.

"The righteous shall live by faith" is equivalent to saying that men shall live by eating. Men are born. They are in this world. The question is, How can they sustain life, become strong, and do their work? The answer is, By eating. Their health will depend upon the quality of their food. Thus is it with Christians. They are born into the spiritual life. How is that life to be sustained and nourished? Paul says they are to live by faith in Christ. Christ says we are to eat his flesh and drink his blood. He explains it by saying that we are to live by him as he lived by the Father. His life was one of obedience, to the last degree of self-sacrifice. Paul says that by his obedience many (or, as the revised version gives it, "the many") shall be made righteous.

How can we apply this law to our daily life and conduct? By keeping in mind that every act of our lives is done from a motive, and that the basis of every motive is either selfishness or the opposite. The opposite of love of self is love of God, even though we may not be fully conscious of it. Our Lord did not say that we must have definite and correct ideas of a Supreme Being, but he did tell us that we must love our fellow-beings. "If ye love not your brother whom ye have seen, how can ye love God, whom ye have not seen?" "Thou shalt love thy neighbor as thyself."

Jesus said that he came to fulfil the law. The epitome of the law as given in the Old Testament is " to deal justly, to love mercy, and to walk humbly before God." Christ's summing of the decalogue was given in the two commands to love God and to love our neighbor.

Love, therefore, is the supreme test of life; and not only of life in general, but of every act of our lives. In that we have our spiritual alchemy, the philosopher's stone, which is to turn the baser metal of our human nature into the divine life, the refined gold, which is to last forever. Love is the basis of that self-denial which Jesus declared to be a necessary qualification of discipleship. Why must we deny self? Because the opposite of self is God, and such denial or emptying of ourselves is the only way of making room for him.

Swedenborg emphasizes with many repetitions and reiterations the truth that the positive work of character-building must come from God, and that our part is to "shun evils as sins." Mary Lyon, the spiritually-minded founder of Mount Holyoke Seminary, frequently called the attention of her pupils to the fact that most of the commandments of the decalogue are in the negative, "Thou shalt *not.*" "God alone," she said, "can work positive results. We can only refrain from evil; he must inspire to good."

Every act of our lives has a spiritual meaning, and makes its impress upon our character for good or ill. Every experience that God sends or permits to enter into our lives is for a definite purpose, and that purpose has reference to the formation of our spiritual natures. If I am a small grocer, and in selling a pound of sugar I deviate from the rule of honesty and good-will to my neighbor, my soul is hurt by it. If I perform the act justly, receiving only a fair and reasonable profit, with a spirit of love in my heart, I gain a grace and my soul expands. It is enabled by that act to take in more of God. If I am a carpenter, and in building a house I exercise my skill faithfully and conscientiously in every particular, being just as careful with the parts that are out of sight as with those that are likely to be observed and criticised; if I rejoice in the privilege of creating a house for my neighbor—in other words, if I put love into my work, I am just as truly building my own soul as building a house. If I labor selfishly, slighting and cheating when it can be done without danger of discovery, I tear down the foundations of my eternal life faster than the material structure rises under my hand. If I am a capitalist and have a talent for accumulating (a talent for building a fortune is just as much God's gift as a talent for building a house), but use the talent for personal ambition or selfish gratification, the destruction of my soul is certain, and the large sums I give in a spirit of ostentation for charitable purposes will not have the slightest effect in retarding my downward spiritual career. If, on the contrary, I rejoice in this talent as a means of increasing my usefulness, if I gather in with the right hand for the sake of giving out with the left, if I act as a faithful steward, striving earnestly to dispense my store in ways that will most truly benefit my fellow-men, then am I "making friends of the mammon of unrighteousness," and laying up treasures in heaven by my loving distribution of riches upon earth.

But it is not only in our occupation or business that we are dealing with eternal things. Every temptation resisted, every evil thought suppressed, every angry or impatient word restrained and unuttered, the slander held back, each and every form of sin or temptation which may assail us, when conquered in the name and strength of the Lord Jesus Christ is a part of the process of burning out the dross of our characters and transmuting them into the spiritual element of which pure gold is the symbol. In and of ourselves we can do nothing of this work. In and through him we can do all things. Day by day the process of self-renunciation must continue "till Christ be formed in us." "Children," said a wise teacher, "here is a beautiful china plate; it is painted with flowers just as charming as they grow. It has been and will be admired by thousands. Every one who observes flowers will be delighted to look at it. But I did not bring it in on account of its beauty. I brought it in to tell you something about its manufacture. First, it is painted; then the colors are burned in. So it is with character: the qualities that make character must be burned in. That is done by trials and temptations. You mean to be truthful; if you are tempted to lie, and resist, you are burning in your truthfulness."

The law of spiritual alchemy was stated by our Saviour in two words—"Deny thyself." This phrase embodies the entire philosophy of eternal life. It describes what is intended to be a supreme and all-inclusive act, a denial of the entire self-nature and all that belongs to it. It is giving up the *ego* and accepting God in its stead. The next phrase, " Take up thy cross and follow me," indicates the application of the general law to particulars. If self is to be given up as a whole, then every part of life must be surrendered.

Spiritual alchemy is, in truth, another name for Divine Providence. It shows how God is dealing with us every moment. It helps us to realize that we are building or destroying, helping or hindering, our spiritual natures by the use we make of every experience of life, however apparently trifling. Spiritual alchemy in our being, like chemistry in the material world, never for a moment ceases its work. As oxygen attacks and strives to destroy every object in nature the moment the life principle leaves it, so does our selfhood, an enemy of eternal vigilance, lie in wait to take possession of every act or thought that is not in accordance with the law of obedience and love. But the principle works equally in our favor when we join ourselves to Christ and seek his life and strength. An earnest writer has given this testimony: " I have noticed that wherever there has been a faithful following of the Lord in a consecrated soul certain results have inevitably followed, sooner or later. Meekness and quietness of spirit become in time the characteristics of the daily life. A submissive acceptance of the will of God as it comes in the hourly events of each day; pliability in the hands of God to do or to suffer all the good pleasure of his will; sweetness under provocation, calmness in the midst of turmoil and bustle, yieldingness to the wishes of others, and an insensibility to slights and affronts; absence of worry or anxiety; deliverance from care and fear—all these, and many similar graces, are invariably found to be the natural outward development of that inward life which is hid with Christ in God."

The Rev. Oliver Dyer relates an incident which illustrates in a most striking way the law of spiritual alchemy, or character-building. It occurred many years ago, while he was living at Lockport, N. Y. He says:

"There was at that time a drunken carpenter in Lockport named A., who was noted for shiftlessness and dishonesty. His wife was an industrious Christian woman who did a good deal of work for the family of a man named M., who was our representative in Congress. The M.'s took a deep interest in Mrs. A., and resolved to give her a permanent home. For that purpose Mr. M. arranged to have a small house built on a lot which he owned in a portion of the village known as Pioneer Hill. Hoping to encourage A., he gave him the job of building the house, without letting him know for what purpose he was having it erected. While M. was absent at Washington A. went on with his work, spinning it out through the fall, winter, and spring, and cheating his employer, both as to the lumber and the work he put into the house, in every way that he possibly could. When M. returned, in the middle of the summer, A. told him that it was all finished in the best style, adding, 'There isn't a better built house on Pioneer Hill than that house of yours.' 'Very well,' said M., 'then you go home and tell Mrs. A. to move into it right away. And here is a deed to her for the property. So you see that you will have a nice house as long as you live.'

"A. took the deed and walked away like one in a dream.

He was dazed at the discovery that, instead of having cheated M., he had been persistently and elaborately engaged for nearly a year in the work of cheating himself. 'Oh, if I'd only known it was my own house that I was building!' he muttered over and over again. He never got over the chagrin occasioned by the discovery of his folly, but felt its sting grow constantly sharper as the defects of the house became more and more apparent with the lapse of time."

In telling this incident the writer adds: "This story always comes to my mind when I am considering the subject of our spiritual house-building; and I am reminded by it how apt people are to cheat themselves in a way which corresponds to the manner in which the unfortunate A. cheated himself. In trying to put unsound lumber or unfaithful work into the house of another, they are surely giving character to their own eternal residence. And the more successful they are in cheating others as to the things of time, the more terribly they cheat themselves as to the things of eternity. 'With what measure ye mete, it shall be measured to you again,' because you measure it to yourself the very moment you mete it to another. Having this eternal and inexorable law in mind, when I think of the miserable A.'s lament over his folly I sometimes shudder as in imagination I seem to hear the cry of some lost spirit as he enters his infernal abode: 'Oh, if I had only known it was my own house that I was building!'"

CHAPTER XV.

SPIRITUAL GROWTH AN UNCONSCIOUS PROCESS.

CAN we be conscious of the growth of the heavenly life in our souls? Can we gage our spiritual development as we do our progress in mathematics or the sciences?

No. It is impossible. The laws of spiritual and mental growth are wholly distinct from each other. It is one of the essential elements of soul scholarship that we cannot know our standing while we are in this probationary or preparatory stage of our being. This is because the spiritual standard is not based upon outward acquirement, but upon motive. Suppose, for instance, a man begins his adult life with such a lack of honesty that he cheats his neighbors in every way he can without falling into the hands of the law. This results so greatly to his disadvantage by leading his neighbors to avoid him that he finally becomes convinced of the unwisdom of the plan. He is led to see that "honesty is the best policy," and gives up his cheating entirely, making it a rule to deal fairly in every case. Instead of being denounced as a rogue, he begins to be quoted as a model of honesty. But has he made any spiritual progress? Has his soul exchanged any of the human element for the divine? Not at all. He has only exercised a deeper shrewdness. He has learned how to serve his self-interest on a broader scale than he did before. Suppose he now begins to extend his thoughts and plans to the future world. He realizes the folly of caring for his interests in this life without giving attention to his welfare in the life to come. He joins the church. Henceforth he is not only strictly honest in his dealings, but he bestows liberal sums in charity. He even visits the poor and relieves the distressed, saying to himself, " I am not going to be so improvident as those people who make all their plans for this world and live as if there were no other existence to provide for. I intend to not only lay up a store for a comfortable old age, but also to provide for the contingencies of the future life."

With such a motive as that, has he yet made any spiritual attainment? None whatever. The Saviour does not teach that we are to cultivate a refined and far-seeing selfishness, but that we are to renounce it altogether. " Deny thyself " is the strait and narrow gate that leads to eternal life—the life of God in the soul. No virtue is a virtue if the motive which prompts it is a latent form of selfishness, a desire to escape condemnation, to win applause, or to secure admission to the place called heaven.

It would be a comfortable state of things and very agreeable to human nature if we could be conscious of our spiritual condition, and know just what progress we are making from day to day. But this would utterly defeat the purpose of our discipline. The school of life would be a failure. The object sought is not merely the cultivation of certain definite faculties, but the union of the entire being with God. Self-knowledge would bring self-complacency. We would be constantly tempted to rest contented with the attainment made, however low the standard might be. But uncertainty forces us directly to God. Knowing the deceitfulness of the human heart, and that we may be under the influence of a hidden motive of selfishness when we are most disposed to be satisfied with ourselves, we have no alternative but to renounce all self-hope, and seek refuge in our Heavenly Father's love. " In our spiritual as in our bodily existence, all vital functions are of divine ordinance and continuance. . . . As by taking thought one cannot add to his stature, which he buildeth not, so can he by no conscious effort contribute directly to his spiritual growth; the increase must come from God."[1]

It is true that this makes life seem difficult, but we are nowhere promised that it shall be easy. On the contrary, it is clearly taught in the Bible that the most prominent elements of the Christian's experience are " fighting, working, and watching." There is no intimation that we are to have in this severe school anything of the nature of a vacation, or even a brief recess. Rest, indeed, is abundantly promised, but it must be obtained *in* the school and not out of it. Our Divine Instructor says, " Come unto *me*, and *I* will give you rest," and there is no promise of gaining it from any other source.

The disposition of human nature to settle down for a comfortable time in this world—to turn the school-house into a play-room—is so strong as to be almost irresistible. But all that is accomplished by other methods would be nullified and the end sought would be entirely frustrated if we were permitted to realize our spiritual progress. George Herbert has expressed the truth in his inimitable way in the following lines:

> When God at first made man,
> Having a glass of blessings standing by,
> " Let us " (said he) " pour on him all we can;
> Let the world's riches, which dispersèd lie,
> Contract into a span."

[1] "God in His World."

So strength first made a way,
Then beauty flowed, then wisdom, honor, pleasure;
When almost all was out, God made a stay,
Perceiving that alone of all his treasure
Rest at the bottom lay.

" For if I should " (said he)
" Bestow this jewel also on my creature,
He would adore my gifts instead of me,
And rest in nature, not the God of nature;
So both would losers be.

" Yet let him keep the rest,
But keep them with repining restlessness;
Let him be rich and weary, that at least,
If goodness lead him not, yet weariness
May toss him to my breast."

Is there then no rest in this world? Yes. Boundless rest; infinite rest. But its source is not here, neither can its satisfactions be derived from the things of time and sense. God is its source, and the degree of our rest and quietness of spirit depends wholly upon the completeness of our union with him. "Thou wilt keep him in perfect peace whose mind is stayed on thee; because he trusteth in thee." Here we have a statement of the entire case— cause and result. Cause, trust in God. Result, peace. This is what is meant by being in the world and yet not of it. If we do our duties faithfully, and trust God in the doing, we not only have rest, but we fulfil the conditions of growth. How we grow, and to what extent, can only be known by him who knows all things. "It doth not yet appear what we shall be."

CHAPTER XVI.

PRAYER IN ITS RELATION TO A UNIVERSAL PROVIDENCE.

"If God has a definite plan for each of us there can be no occasion for prayer." This argument is sometimes advanced, but it is utterly groundless. It is quite true that there is no occasion for many of the prayers that are offered; but for genuine prayer there can be no foundation like that furnished by a belief in Divine Providence.

In the first place, it gives us a perfect Father to answer our prayers. Suppose an earthly father sends his son to a distant school, promising that, while he seems to be far away, he will yet keep constant watch over him, will supply all his needs, and overrule for his good the various experiences through which he may pass. Would that imply that he was never to ask his father for anything? Would it not be far more natural for the father to say, "In order to help you in the best way, it will be necessary for you to keep in constant communication with me, to tell me all your troubles, and ask freely for everything you want. But in doing this you must remember that I am the one to judge what is for your real advantage and welfare. While in school it is impossible for you to know this. With your requests, therefore, I hope to always see evidence that you have confidence in my judgment and my love, and that you accept cheerfully what I send in answer to your petitions." This is just what is implied in the injunctions, "Ask, and ye shall receive," "Seek *first* my kingdom." And thus we find that with all the earnest and agonizing prayers of the Son of God was linked the invariable word of submission, "Not my will, but thine, be done."

Mr. C. T. Porter, in his remarkable book "Mechanics and Faith," offers this striking definition: "Prayer is the highest form of coöperative action required on the part of man." He also says: "Prayer is the mode of effort that is adapted to the nature of the spiritual good that is sought by it, as labor and study are modes of effort that are adapted to the inferior goods we seek. Labor and study are practical modes of asking for what we seek by them; a way of putting our minds into a receptive condition. So with prayer."

There can be no difficulty in reconciling prayer with the theory of a divine plan when it is remembered that the Author of the plan instructs us to pray, and therefore *his plan must include our prayers*. But they must be right prayers and in a right spirit. They must never be *demands*. He who has the most of the spirit of prayer will be least disposed to press his own wishes. Having laid his petitions before the all-wise and all-loving Father, he will rest peacefully in the one desire that embraces and absorbs all others—"Not my will, but thine, be done."

They must also be *trustful* prayers. If we ask for guidance in the difficult ways of our daily life we must believe that he is so guiding us, however dark the pathway may seem to us. There was profound philosophy in the remark of a child in connection with the sad fate of President Garfield. The following conversation between two little girls was overheard:

"I am sure President Garfield will get well, because people are praying for him all over the world."

"*I* don't feel sure of it."

"What! Don't you believe that God answers prayer?"

"Oh, yes! I *know* that God answers prayer. He *always* answers prayer, but *sometimes he answers yes, and sometimes he answers no.*"

One of the scriptural injunctions to prayer which we find it hard to take literally is that it shall be continual. "Pray without ceasing." Since we cannot spend all our time upon our knees or in what we regard as the special religious exercise of prayer, we dismiss this plain direction as hyperbolical. But it is not. It is a clear instruction that we are to have a spirit of prayer in all that we do. There is no act of our lives so trifling that it does not come within the scope of God's plan. The spirit of prayer will therefore lead us to "pray without ceasing" that God's will may be done in the smallest particulars of our lives. The desire to do his will *is* a prayer. It does not need expression in words every moment, nor even "the upward lifting of an eye." The desire to act for God and not for self is a practical expression of the petition "Thy will be done" in every act that is thus consecrated.

It must not be forgotten that the foundation of prayer is God's love and his infinite desire to do all things for us. There are no limitations on his side, but there are very many on ours. We must not think of him as a great, inconceivable Being somewhere in space who must be induced to "lend a listening ear" to our supplications, with a hope that after a careful consideration of the case he may decide to grant our request. He is not far, but near.

Faber says: "He is not so far as even to be near." He is within us and a part of us, if we will but allow it. His relation to us may be compared to the atmosphere. We cannot keep it out of our lungs as long as we have life. Yet how often the "prayer of invocation" at the opening of religious service has the effect of placing God at a distance. "We lift up our eyes unto thee," "Thou hast taught us to draw near thee," "We beseech thee to lend a listening ear as we bring thee our prayers and praises"—such petitions may often be heard.

Suppose we imagine ourselves praying in the same way to the air we breath. "We beseech thee, O Atmosphere, to come into our lungs and give us health and strength. Our blood needs to be purified, that it may carry its life-giving power to every part of our body," etc. There is room for a long and eloquent plea on this line. We are too wise to do this on the physical plane. We know well that in order to secure physical blessings we must exercise "the highest form of coöperative action" of which we are capable. We expand the chest and inhale the air we need, knowing that it is only waiting for an opportunity to come into our bodies to bless them. If our lungs are weak, we inhale more air as the natural way of strengthening them. When we learn to pray for God as our lungs pray for air, there will be no trouble about our spiritual life and health.

F. W. Robertson says: "That prayer which does not succeed in moderating our wish, in changing the passionate desire into still submission, the anxious, tumultuous expectation into silent surrender, is no true prayer, and proves that we have not the spirit of true prayer. That life is most holy in which there is the least of petition and desire, and most of waiting upon God; that in which petition most often passes into thanksgiving. Pray till prayer makes you forget your own wish, and leave it or merge it in God's will. The divine wisdom has given us prayer not as a means whereby to obtain the good things of earth, but as a means whereby we learn to do without them; not as a means whereby we escape evil, but as a means whereby we become strong to meet it."

One of the most noteworthy answers to prayer of which we have any record affords a lesson which is usually overlooked. God told Solomon that he might ask for what he wished. He asked for wisdom. Then God said: "Because thou hast *not* asked for riches, wealth, or honor, nor the life of thine enemies, behold, I have done according to thy words, and I have also given thee that which thou hast *not* asked."

But prayer is not limited to petition. It is also communion. What would we think of a friend who never sought our society except when he had a favor to ask? However conscious we may be of the continual presence of God, there will be times when we wish to turn aside from "the cares that infest the day" and hold special fellowship with our Lord.

The true spirit of prayer is founded upon a complete trust in Divine Providence. It involves a full surrender of ourselves to God, and a willingness to be, to do, or to suffer whatever he sees to be best for us. The prayer "Thy will be done" does not mean that we are to become nothing, but that we are to become everything. To make our wills identical with God's will is to make ourselves a medium for accomplishing his divine and eternal purposes. "By obedience we take on all the resources of God," says Dr. George D. Herron.

The Rev. Samuel M. Crothers, writing on prayer, quotes the poet's words,

> God is seen God
> In the star, in the stone, in the flesh, in the
> soul and the clod.

and comments as follows:

"God is God in the star! All silent, we bow down before the glory unapproachable, the light ineffable. No cry of ours can cross the mighty spaces. But God is God in the soul, and to the God in the soul the soul cries for help. 'Out of the depths do I cry unto thee!' It is the deep calling unto deep; the deep of need calling to the deep of power—that is prayer.

"And does such prayer come from a weakness of will? Rather it is the very highest exercise of will. It is not the casting aside of our proper burden; it is the calling of all that is within us to aid us in bearing that burden. And it is based upon the belief that we have not summoned all that is within us till we have called upon the God who is working in us. For

> Deep below the deeps of conscious being
> Thy splendor shineth: there, O God, thou art.

"When thus we pray, 'Thy kingdom come,' we mean that our hearts' desire is that that kingdom should come in us and through us. It is the opening of the gates of our souls that the King of Glory may come in. The prayer 'Thy will be done' means, first of all, that we stand ready to do his will. The prayer 'Give us this day our daily bread' is not the idle petition of the sluggard, for it must be answered 'according to the power that worketh in us.'

"The attitude of prayer is not that of the ship-master who, with anchor cast and every sail furled, simply wishes himself in another haven. It is itself the lifting of the anchor and the spreading of the sail. It is each white sail crying, 'Fill us, O winds of God, and we together shall cross the seas.'

"But if divine power works in us, would it not work alike whether we desire it or not? Does our prayer change anything? I think we will find that the condition of receiving the highest good is that we seek it and ask for it. There are certain functions of life that go on automatically, but the higher functions rise into the region of consciousness and intelligent coöperation. The man ceases to be a blind instrument, and becomes a servant and at last a friend of God. It is enough for the tool that it lies, without will of its own, in the master's hand. The slave may serve in sullen silence, but he who feels himself to be a fellow-laborer with God seeks to commune with him. The best gifts come not unsought, and love is doubly manifested in the grace of asking and the grace of giving.

"The goodliest guests do not force themselves upon us. They stand at the door and knock, and only when we open the door do they come in to us. We have life, but whether we shall have a deeper and more abundant life depends upon how sincerely we desire it. There are lives depressed below the level of the universal life, like the Dead Sea and the parched deserts, which lie below the level of the ocean. But the Dead Sea lies below the ocean-level because it is shut out from connection with it. Once open a channel, and from remotest shores great waves would roll toward it till it would be filled. If our lives are empty in a universe full of joy and power, it is because we have allowed the channels through which the most blessed influences might flow to us to become choked. Conscious prayer is the opening of our hearts, that the tides of divine power may flow through us."

CHAPTER XVII.

TO WHAT EXTENT ARE WE RESPONSIBLE FOR OTHERS?

THIS is often a perplexing question. We may be willing to trust God for ourselves, but how can we be contented and restful when evils threaten our children or dear friends? There is but one law for the Christian under every circumstance, and that is the law of *trust*. Having done what we can for children, for friends, for the poor, we must leave them in the hands of the loving Father, "who doeth all things well."

When friends fall into trouble we long to help them, and wonder why we are not allowed to have the means to carry them the relief they so much need. In reality we wish to be a *providence* to them. We would shield them from the trials which, as God has permitted them, must be the form of discipline they especially require. We need to trust his wisdom for them as we do for ourselves.

Trusting for others is, in some respects, harder than trusting for ourselves. This is especially true in the case of those for whom we feel a deep responsibility. Loving parents find it hard to be restful when troubles come upon their children. To believe that God has not forgotten, that his love is greater than their own, that his wisdom sees some experiences to be necessary for their children that they would do all in their power to shield them from—

this is a severe test of faith. The conscientious teacher is placed in a somewhat similar relation to the children under his charge. He feels a deep responsibility for them, yet there are so many influences entirely beyond his control. The only refuge is *trust*. God's care is universal. We cannot love our children, pupils, or friends as much as he loves them, and his love is guided by perfect wisdom and with a full knowledge of circumstances and conditions of which we are entirely ignorant. The Saviour tells us to cast *all* our cares upon him, and responsibility for others must necessarily be included with the rest. If we have the right motive, a desire to do our duty, to find out God's will and to do it, we may have full confidence that he will use us, and that he is the best judge as to the way and the extent to which our efforts can be utilized.

The question for the earnest Christian to consider is not, How many of the unconverted can I speak to to-day? but, How can I most completely surrender myself to God's will, and thus be used for the accomplishment of his purpose? His plan comprehends all things, even our casual meeting with people day by day and the influence we are to give and receive. It may be that there will not be for us to-day a single one of what are regarded as distinctively religious duties. Yet some simple act of honesty, some work faithfully performed, may make an impression on an unsuspected observer which will give him a new idea of Christian living and change the whole current of his life. When Peter went into the sepulchre he simply obeyed the law of his nature, which was all impulse and energy. He had no thought whatever of performing a " religious duty." Yet what was the consequence? "Then went in also that other disciple, which came first to the sepulcher, and he saw and believed." John outran Peter, and arrived at the sepulcher first. But he only *looked* in, and for some reason his faith was not touched by what he saw. Peter, with his characteristic eagerness, went in as soon as he arrived, and John was induced by his example to enter also. Thus he was led to *believe*, and was fully prepared to bear witness to one evidence of our Lord's resurrection. Dr. Horace Bushnell made this incident the subject of one of his noblest sermons, in which he emphasized the truth that our " unconscious influence " is sometimes far more potent than the active efforts which occupy our attention so fully, and from which our narrow vision leads us to expect such great results. Let us listen to Emerson's wise words in the same direction:

"A little consideration of what takes place around us every day would show us that a higher law than that of our will regulates events; that our painful labors are unnecessary and fruitless; that only in our easy, simple, spontaneous action are we strong, and by contenting ourselves with obedience we become divine. Belief and love —a believing love—will relieve us of a vast load of care. O my brothers, God exists. There is a soul at the center of nature and over the will of every man, so that none of us can wrong the universe. It has so infused its strong enchantment into nature that we prosper when we accept its advice; and when we struggle to wound its creatures, our hands are glued to our sides, or they beat our own breasts. The whole course of things goes to teach us faith. We need only obey. There is guidance for each of us, and by lowly listening we shall hear the right word. Why need you choose so painfully your place and occupation and associates, and modes of action and of entertainment?

Certainly there is a possible right for you that precludes the need of balance and wilful election. For you there is a reality, a fit place and congenial duties. Place yourself in the middle of the stream of power and wisdom which animates all whom it floats, and you are without effort impelled to truth, to right, and a perfect contentment. Then you put all gainsayers in the wrong. Then you are the world, the measure of right, of truth, of beauty. If we will not be marplots with our miserable interferences, the work, the society, letters, arts, science, religion of men would go on far better than now, and the heaven predicted from the beginning of the world, and still predicted from the bottom of the heart, would organize itself as do now the rose and the air and the sun."

CHAPTER XVIII.

SOME DARK PROBLEMS.

A THEORY of the universe with an Infinite Being to create and superintend it is difficult. A theory of the universe without such a Being is impossible. Men may claim to hold that theory as one might foolishly assert that his life is not sustained by the atmosphere, but down in the depths of every human soul there is a demand for God as truly as the lungs demand air. The anarchist was involuntarily true to his own nature who said: " I have succeeded in ridding myself of all my former ideas and notions about a Supreme Being, *thank God.*"

There are certain dark problems pertaining to human life which naturally suggest themselves when the subject of Divine Providence is under consideration. The more prominent of these difficulties will now be briefly discussed.

THE CRUELTY OF NATURE'S LAWS.

When this is advanced as an argument against a universal and beneficent providence the only answer required is a simple denial. Nature's laws are not cruel. The suffering they cause among men is not the result of the laws, but of their violation. The law of gravitation is often spoken of as cruel because a fall may occasion injury or death. But the law is wholly wise and good. Its seeming cruelty in the fact that it is inexorable is one of its most valuable characteristics. Suppose it were otherwise, and there were exceptions to the law that falling will hurt, or putting the hand in the fire will burn, or taking poison will cause suffering and death. What confusion and chaos would result! The mind would be confounded, stultified. No plans could be formed and no enterprises carried out. The certainty of nature's laws affords the only basis for a rational or organized life in the world. All we can ask the Author of the laws in addition is to superintend his children in the use of them, and this is exactly what he promises to do.

SUFFERING AMONG ANIMALS.

"How can a loving God create animals to devour each other by the million?" is a favorite question of the skeptic. But what would the critic do if he could rearrange the universe to his mind? Would he dispense with the animal kingdom entirely? That would make a strange world of it. An element would be omitted which we cannot but regard as essential to the completeness of human life and experience. Granting, then, the necessity of animal life in the world, what improvement can we imagine in the manner of its production or its fate?

Doubtless the first thought of many would be to banish all fierce and venomous animals and insects. Yet there is much to be considered before the wisdom of that step can be conceded. The earth is our school-house, and all of nature's varied productions are a part of the apparatus for our education. If the dove and the lamb are required to convey lessons of gentleness and innocence, do we not equally need the tiger and the serpent to illustrate the opposite tendencies of human nature? It is a striking and highly suggestive truth that every phase of human capacity has its counterpart in the animal kingdom. The noble horse, the soaring eagle, the industrious ant, the cunning fox, the lazy sloth, the greedy hog, the venomous snake, the plotting spider setting traps for the unwary—every manifestation of human character finds some expression among the lower orders of creation. Are there not even some people who sting our souls as gnats do our bodies?

If all the object-lessons of nature are essential to the complete education of the human race, the question next arises, Could not the animal world exist with much less suffering than now appears?

In answering this inquiry we must first consider the laws that are already in operation, and see whether they contribute to the desired result, and to what extent.

Mr. Alfred Russel Wallace, who wrought out a theory of evolution at the same time with Darwin, though unconscious of Darwin's plan, and who presented an essay on Natural Selection to the Linnean Society of London as early as 1858, has treated the subject of cruelty in the animal world at some length in a later work entitled "Darwinism: An Exposition of the Theory of Natural Selection, with some of its Applications." He says: "There is, I think, good reason to believe that all this is greatly exaggerated; that the supposed 'torments' and 'miseries' of animals have little real existence, but are the reflection of the imagined sensations of cultivated men and women in similar circumstances, and that the amount of actual suffering caused by the struggle for existence among animals is altogether insignificant." He argues the question at considerable length. The conclusions to be deduced from his statements and those of other close observers of nature may be summarized as follows:

1. Animals are free from one of the most prominent elements of suffering among human beings, namely, dread, or anticipation.

2. In a great majority of cases, especially among insects and the smaller animals, death is instantaneous and painless.

3. When death does not occur at once, there is reason to believe that the nerves are hypnotized or partially paralyzed, and the sensibility to pain is destroyed. A cat playing with a mouse appears to produce the very refinement of suffering. Yet men who have been caught by fierce animals and treated in the same way testify that the distress is only in appearance. Livingstone was once captured by a lion, and afterward described his sensations with all particulars. The lion first seized him and shook him as a cat always does on catching a mouse or rat. This had the effect to so deaden his sensibilities that he lost all suffering both from pain and fear. He retained his consciousness, and when the lion released him in the feline way of playing with its prey, he made an instinctive or mechanical effort to escape, but had no sense of either physical or mental distress.

His testimony, which is fully confirmed by others who have passed through a similar experience, is of the utmost value in considering the question of nature's cruelty. It leads to a natural and legitimate inference that all the apparent suffering of animals is mitigated in a similar way.

It must be remembered that the nervous systems of the lower orders of animals are essentially different from ours. It is well known that fish, after being caught with a " cruel hook," will often return at once to the bait, showing that the sense of hunger is stronger than that of pain. Even the horse, whose high-strung nerves seem closely akin to those of man, sometimes gives surprising evidence of dull sensibility to pain. Mr. Wallace quotes examples of this in his book.

The Bible affords many indications of God's care for his dumb creatures. If an ox fell into a pit it must be delivered, even though it required a violation of the strict laws regarding the Jewish sabbath. When God gave his reasons to Jonah for wishing to spare Nineveh he not only mentioned its six score thousand inhabitants, but "also much cattle." It is a singular fact, and perhaps not often observed, that the Saviour's message after his resurrection was, " Go into all the world and preach the gospel to every *creature*" (in the new version, " to the whole creation "). The horse who takes his master to church very Sunday little suspects that the message delivered there is one of mercy to himself. The Rev. Rowland Hill said : " I would not give a farthing for a man's religion if his dog and cat are not the better off for it."

From these various considerations it is reasonable to conclude that the appearance of suffering among animals is largely deceptive. The expression " survival of the fittest" has a harsh and cruel sound. It appears to indicate what Mr. Laing describes as " these cruel internecine battles between individuals and species in the struggle for existence." At first thought it seems directly opposed to the theory of a beneficent providence in the world. But a more thorough consideration shows the law to be in reality a mandate of mercy. The animals that are overcome and slain in the struggle with their stronger fellows are often thus spared a slow and lingering death from starvation and weakness.

It is no exhibition of wisdom nor even of a reasonable sympathy to accuse the Divine Creator of cruelty in the realm of "animated nature." The more we know of the secret laws of that realm the more we are enabled to realize that infinite love reigns there as it does everywhere else, and that all possible mitigating influences are employed to destroy or diminish the pain which must necessarily exist in a world of selfishness and sin. Many sparrows may be permitted to fall to the ground, but not one can do so without the knowledge and care of the Infinite Father.

THE SUFFERINGS OF CHILDREN.

This theme appeals to the universal human heart. No one whose soul is lighted with a single ray of sympathy can walk through the squalid districts of a great city without deep emotions of pity and sorrow for the swarms of wretched children that are always to be seen there. No other sight can more surely challenge our faith in Divine Providence than this. Why must innocent children suffer so terribly for the idleness, the folly, the crimes of their parents? Where is the beneficence of the inexorable law which sends three or four times as many little ones into the hovels of the poor as into the mansions of the rich? Such are the questions which force themselves upon us and will not be satisfied without an answer.

It is useless to expect a complete solution of this difficult problem, but it is our duty and privilege to study it profoundly and see if we cannot discover laws and principles which indicate a Father's care even in this, the darkest side of human history.

In the first place, it must be noted that a part of the supposed sufferings are the creations of our own deeply moved feelings. Mr. Wallace's sentence regarding the sufferings of animals applies equally in this case. Our feelings are to some extent "the reflection of the imagined sensations of cultivated men and women in similar circumstances." We are repelled, for instance, by dirt, but little children are not troubled by it. In fact, they enjoy the ways of dirt more than the ways of cleanliness, as all careful mothers well know. When we see children playing in a filthy alley or court we naturally call to mind a similar group in the country, and pity the "poor little wretches" for having no grass or flowers to enjoy. But they have not been accustomed to country scenes and privileges, and have no sense of deprivation or loss. It has been remarked in the beautiful work of the "fresh-air fund" that the poor little waifs in many cases do not go into raptures over fields and grass and flowers as their enthusiastic patrons expect them to. Their sense of the beautiful in nature has not been cultivated; and it cannot spring into being in a moment. They have been mercifully adapted to their environment.

Another appeal to our sympathies, and a very strong one, arises from the coarseness and oftentimes the brutality of their treatment in their rude homes. Two modifying principles apply here—dulness and forgetfulness. The sensibilities become blunted. Harsh words lose their power to wound. If they can escape without blows they are well content. Then they easily forget. An adult would suffer from a rankling sense of injustice under such treatment, but the child lives in the present moment. It quickly forgets the sorrows of the past, and has not the dread of the future which belongs to the adult mind.

It is true that there is an element of sadness in these very safeguards against a child's unhappiness. It is painful to see its sensibilities blunted, its love of the beautiful undeveloped. But we must take the problem as we find it. We must study it in its broadest aspects. We must, as far as possible, try to see it as God sees it. His purpose is the creation of a race of immortal beings endowed with qualities similar to his own, which qualities are made personal and individual by a freedom of choice between good and evil, and by the discipline which grows out of that freedom, inasmuch as some degree of evil is sure to result from the privilege of choice. The question we have to consider is not that of suffering *per se*, which is God's problem and not ours, but whether we can discern clear evidences of a loving supervision which does all that can be done to mitigate the suffering without so interfering with man's freedom as to destroy his individuality. Some of the tokens of such a supervision have already been mentioned. But there are darker shadows still unrelieved. Squalor and dirt, comfortless homes and unkind parents, do not indicate the limit of childhood's sufferings. Hunger, starvation, cruel blows, painful and lingering disease— which latter may come to the rich equally with the poor— what modifying law do we find for these terrible evils to show a Heavenly Father's kind remembrance?

One such law can be stated at once—the law of removal. Millions of children are taken every year from the trials of this world to the pure and perfect enjoyments of the next. Why others are left to endure privations and hardships for a longer season we do not know. We are not required to know. But we *are* required to believe that the Divine Being, whose plan embraces eternity, is a better judge than we can be of the highest permanent good of each individual. Doubtless the influence of childhood cannot be spared from the homes of the degraded and the outcast. We are taught that angelic ministrations accompany little children. "In heaven their angels do always behold the face of my Father which is in heaven." If there is so much hardness and cruelty in the homes of the lower classes now, what would be the history with the element of childhood omitted? We do not know how many crimes are prevented by the coming of a babe into the home.

THE POVERTY OF THE MASSES.

The sum of wretchedness among the masses is an appalling thought to every lover of his kind. But it should not rob us of our trust in a Heavenly Father's goodness unless we are sure we understand the case exactly as he understands it. Do we know what is to become of earth's untold millions in the future life? Our theological system has consigned them to the lower regions by the decrees of an inexorable logic. But we are beginning to realize that our whole process of reasoning may have been fallacious; that the substitution of an immanent for an external God may necessitate a modification of all our views of religious truth and the basis of man's salvation.

Two pregnant facts are to be noted in this connection. The first is, at least in the present stage of human evolution, the evident purpose of God that the great majority of the race shall be poor. The law of generation, which ordains large families for the poor and small ones for the rich, has already been alluded to. The second fact to be mentioned seems to have no connection with the first, yet it may be found, on closer examination, to have a most distinct and vital relation to it—the infinite tenderness manifested by our Lord when upon the earth toward the weaknesses and frailties of human nature. It was expressly prophesied concerning him centuries before his advent, " A bruised reed shall he not break, and smoking flax shall he not quench." This was fulfilled in all the varied forms of his ministry to human needs. The Pharisees expected him to join them in their defense of rites, ceremonies, and ecclesiasticism, but he preferred to be a " friend of publicans and sinners," and for this he was condemned to death. The only sin that invariably called forth his fiery indignation and unsparing censure was self-righteousness. Now, is not that the sin which is least likely to be found among the poor and the degraded? Every other form of evil may exist among them; but a belief in their own goodness—that latent poison which is so fatal to the soul because it shuts out God—for that temptation there is little room. The more we study the character and life of Christ, and see how far modern society has separated itself from his precepts, the more we shall be inclined to believe that the people who are most to be pitied are not the poor and the wretched, but the well-to-do, including all of us who have comfortable homes and agreeable friends and so much in our circumstances to tempt us into adapting ourselves to this pleasant world. Judging by our Lord's standard, it certainly appears that the temptations which grow out of our condition are more subtle and dangerous than the temptations of the wretchedly poor. If by their trials and sufferings the spirit of self-righteousness is crushed out of them, and they are thus made to feel their need of God, is not their state more desirable than that of those who say, " Lord, Lord," and do not the things that he says?

This is a subject about which no one has a right to dogmatize. It is also one with regard to which no Christian can be indifferent. The truths that may be taken as a guide to our thoughts and a foundation of hope for the masses are the following:

1. God's love is infinite.

2. He will use every means to save his children that will not interfere with their freedom of choice.

3. All the riches of the earth are his, yet he permits a great majority of the human race to be poor.

4. We must therefore conclude that the condition of poverty is best for their eternal welfare.

5. He indicates ministry to the poor as among the most important duties of those who profess to follow him.

6. Hence we must further conclude that the problem of human poverty is intended to involve and affect the spiritual welfare of the well-to-do and the rich as well as that of the poor themselves.

THE FATE OF THE HEATHEN.

The fate of the heathen has always been regarded as one of the most unsolvable of the " dark problems " of human life and destiny. The theoretical " plan," based on pitiless logic, had no provision and no hope for the millions who have not heard of Christ, and who therefore can have no " saving faith " in him. Happily this iron-clad system, which served a very useful purpose during a certain stage of the world's religious history, is yielding to new forms of belief of which love and not logic is the corner-stone. The newer trend of thought is expressed in the following paragraph:

"The modern science of Comparative Religion has made men wiser in making them more catholic. It has made them more scriptural in making them more charitable in their judgments. We are beginning to learn that God has not left himself without a witness in any nation or any age; that the laws written on two tables of stone were simply clear and definite interpretations of the laws written on the universal conscience; that the unveiling of God which we call Revelation was not confined to the Jewish people; that some knowledge both of the law and of the Lawgiver has been afforded in all times and to all peoples. We are beginning to recognize that Melchizedek, the unknown prophet of what we call Natural Religion, has had his parallel in many lands; that Confucius, Buddha, Socrates, Mohammed, were not emissaries of the devil, but prophets of the Most High God; that, in short, wherever any man has endeavored to heal the broken-hearted, proclaim deliverance to the captives and recovering of sight to the blind, and to set at liberty them that are oppressed, it is because in some measure the Spirit of the Lord God has been upon him, and has anointed him to preach glad tidings to the people. This seems to us to be the spirit which underlies Paul's sermon upon Mars Hill."[1]

This cannot be regarded as heresy, for it is in accordance with the teachings of the early Christian fathers. Justin Martyr, writing in the second century, says: "One

[1] The *Christian Union*, March 20, 1890.

article of our faith is that Christ is the first-begotten of God, and we have already proved him to be the very Logos, or Universal Reason, of which mankind are all partakers, and therefore those who live according to the Logos are Christians, notwithstanding they may pass with you for atheists. Such among the Greeks were Socrates and Herakleitos."

Clement said in the third century: "It is clear that the same God to whom we owe the Old and New Testaments gave also to the Greeks their Greek philosophy."

St. Augustine writes thus in the fourth century: "If the Gentiles also had possibly something divine and true in their doctrines, our saints did not find fault with it. The Apostle Paul, when he said something about God among the Athenians, quoted the testimony of the Greeks, who had something of the same kind."

Religious systems which existed centuries before the advent of the Divine Man embody sentiments and precepts which inculcate the highest morality. In the Zend Avesta of the Persians there are many sentences like the following:

"I keep forever purity and good-mindedness; teach thou me, Ahura Mazda, out of thyself from heaven by thy mouth, whereby the world first arose."

"We honor the good spirit, the good kingdom, the good law, all that is good."

The Buddhist precepts are numerous, of which a few are given:

"Conquer anger by mildness, evil by good, falsehood by truth."

"Be not desirous of discovering the faults of others, but zealously guard your own."

"He is a more noble warrior who subdues himself than he who in battle conquers thousands."

"To the virtuous all is pure. Therefore think not that going unclothed, fasting, or lying on the ground can make the impure pure, for the mind will still remain the same."

The difference between the other religions and Christianity is stated with wise discrimination by Dr. James Freeman Clark: "In the former, man is struggling upward to find God. In Christianity God comes down to find man." Yet even this beautiful saying must be taken with some degree of limitation. God in reality comes down to find man in all religions, but he can only give the world what it is prepared to receive in various stages of advancement. Dr. Lyman Abbott says: "I suppose we have all, at times, wondered that God does not make a clearer revelation of himself. If there be a God, why does he not make it perfectly clear that there is, so that I cannot doubt it? But did it ever occur to you that this may be impossible, even for God? It is very difficult to find a human soul. It may be just as difficult for God to find us as it is for us to find God. Undertake to get the attention of a class of Sunday-school children, and while you talk see how this one looks off with a vacant stare about the room."

At a certain point of moral and religious development of the race God came in person to give the world a revelation of his truth, i.e., of himself, yet even that was not a full revelation. It was the beginning of a full revelation. He was obliged to say to his nearest disciples, "I have many things to say to you, but ye cannot bear them now." Light has been flowing into the minds of his followers ever since, and never with such fulness as at the present time.

Bishop Clark of Rhode Island relates the following incident: "Something like fifty years ago the Rev. William Jones Boone, as he was about to sail for China, where he became our first missionary bishop, delivered in my church in Boston a very impassioned and fervent discourse in behalf of the work to which he had dedicated his life; in the course of which he urged, as the overpowering motive in behalf of his mission, the awful fact that, while we were neglecting our duty, there were so many thousands of Chinamen—specifying the number—who were every hour sinking down into everlasting and irremediable perdition. On his return to this country some years after, I alluded to that sermon. He replied in a very positive way: 'I have changed my mind about that. I had a very valuable Chinese servant in my employ upon whom I leaned with implicit confidence. One day he came to me and said, "I shall be obliged to ask you to find some one to take my place, as in the course of a few weeks I am to be executed in place of a rich gentleman who is to pay me very liberally for becoming his substitute"—such an exchange, as the reader may know, being in accordance with the law of the Empire. I inquired what possible inducement there could be for him to forfeit his life for any amount of money. He replied: "I have an aged father and mother who are very poor and unable to work, and the money that I am to receive will make them comfortable as long as they live. I think it is my duty to give up my life for the sake of accomplishing this."'"

The bishop added: "I could hardly make up my mind to believe that a man who was going into the other world from such a motive as this would be consigned to eternal torment."

A reverent consideration of the laws of Divine Providence in relation to the condition and fate of the heathen should lead us to humbler views of ourselves and to less dogmatism about them. When one of the natives of South Africa kills a sheep or a bullock he invites all the neighbors to come and share it with him. When the missionary who goes there to Christianize them kills an animal, he salts it and stores it away for his own future use. Are the people to be blamed for calling him " stingy "? If the missionary should try to prove that his way is in accordance with the instructions of his Lord and Master, he would find he had undertaken a difficult task.

The Rev. Robert Hamill Nassau, D.D., M.D., for many years a missionary to the West Coast tribes, says:

> After more than thirty years' residence among these tribes, I am able unhesitatingly to say that, among all the many degraded ones with whom I have met, I have seen or heard of none whose religious thought was only a superstition. Standing in the village street surrounded by a company whom the chief has courteously summoned at my request, when I say to him, " I have come to speak to your people," I do not need to begin by telling them there is a God. Looking on that motley assemblage of villagers—the bold, gaunt cannibal with his armament of gun, spear, and dagger; the artisan with rude adz in hand, or hands soiled at the antique bellows of the village smithy; women who have hasted from their kitchen fire with hands white with the manioc dough, or still grasping the partly scaled fish; and children checked in their play, with tiny bow and arrow, or startled from their dusty street pursuit of dog or goat—I have yet to be asked, " Who is God? " Under the slightly varying form of "Anyambie," "Anyambe," " Njambi," " Nzambi," "Anzam," " Nyam," or, in other parts, as " Ukuku," " Suku," etc., they know of a Being superior to themselves, of whom they say to me that he is their " Maker" and " Father." The divine and human relations of these two names at once gave me ground on which to stand in beginning my address.
>
> If, suddenly, they should be asked the question, " Do you know Anyambe ?" they would probably tell any white visitor, trader, traveler, or even missionary, under a feeling of their general ignorance and the white man's superior knowledge, " No; what do *we* know? You white people are spirits; you came from Anyambe's Town and know all about him." (This will help

to explain what is probably true, that some natives may have sometimes made the thoughtless admission that they "knew nothing about a God.") I reply, "No; I am not a spirit, and while I do indeed know about Anyambe, I did not call him by that name. It's your own word. Where did you get it?" "Our forefathers told us that name. Nzambi is the One who made us; he is our Father." Pursuing the conversation, they will interestingly and voluntarily say, "He made these trees," under an immense variety of circumstances, with the most varied of audiences, and before extremes of ignorance, savagery, and uncivilization, utterly barring out the admission of a probability that the tribe, audience, or individual in question had obtained some previous knowledge of the name by hearsay from adjacent more enlightened tribes. For the *name* of the Great Being was everywhere, and in every tribe, varied in form by the difference belonging to their own tribe, and not imported from others; for where tribes are hundreds of miles apart, or their dialectic differences great, the variation in the name is great, i.e., "Suku" of the Bihe country south of the Congo, and "Nzam," of the cannibal Fang north of the equator.

Dr. R. R. Meredith touches the key-note in these burning sentences: "When we see the pagan bowing before his fetich, we are apt to say, 'Oh this terrible degradation of paganism!' But drop your line ten thousand fathoms deeper and see the soul-feeling after God and then you will say, 'Oh the divine dignity of man! You cannot make him forget God, and if he can have no better, he whittles one out of a block of wood.' And in this is the basis of all hope for the salvation of man. God is the Father of every last man on the face of the earth."

PUBLIC CALAMITIES.

The imagination is always strongly impressed by large proportions. Hence a great disaster, affecting many people —a flood, a cyclone, or an earthquake—has a startling effect upon the public mind. The thoughtless and inconsiderate are stirred as they could be by nothing else. Many who scarcely think of God from the beginning to the end of the year are suddenly led to realize that there is such a Being, and begin to question his ways. "Can he be good and permit such terrible things to happen?"

One truth is rarely thought of, although it removes nearly all the difficulties of the case in relation to the question of Divine Providence. The magnitude of the calamity is perceived only by the outside world and is of little or no concern to the individual sufferers. If a single person is burned to death or falls from a bridge and is drowned, it is just as much a solemn and eternal experience to him as if a large hotel were destroyed by fire with a thousand inmates, or a great bridge gave way precipitating many hundreds of people into the water. The question of "providence" belongs as much to one case as to the other. This aspect of the subject affords, in reality, all the solution the problem requires, as far as it is a problem. But one fallacy should be carefully avoided. Even those who express faith in a Divine Providence ruling all events sometimes speak as if a few may be sacrificed for the good of the many. This idea is pagan and not Christian. If a community or a nation is sometimes taught a lesson by a shocking calamity, the sufferers through whom the lesson is conveyed are just as much the objects of God's fatherly care as are the many who escape. Not one life is taken, not one family circle is broken, not one bruised and maimed body remains to suffer, except as a part of the infinite educational plan of the All-seeing One who is guiding each of his creatures in the current of an eternal purpose.

GENERAL REMARKS CONCERNING DARK PROBLEMS.

To an open and candid mind the fact that some human experiences cannot be fully understood is no argument, and cannot be made the basis of an argument, against God or the beneficence of his works. That his view embraces eternity while ours is limited to a brief space of time is reason enough for a suspension of judgment on our part. It would be a sufficient reason even if we were unable to discern evidences of a modifying influence working for the amelioration of human ills. But such evidences are apparent in a thousand forms. The Bible is full of them. The Book of Leviticus sets forth the grandest system of philanthropy that was ever known. It left no room for pauperism, for the simple reason that it was based on justice. The needs of the poor were recognized as *rights*. "When ye reap the harvest of the land, thou shalt not make clean riddance of the corners of thy field when thou reapest, neither shalt thou gather any gleaning of thy harvest: thou shalt leave them unto the poor, and to the stranger: I am the Lord thy God."[1]

One form of injustice in the dealings of the rich with the poor is delaying the payment of wages after they are earned. The divine plan as given to the Jews forestalled that evil by requiring immediate payment of whatever was due. Not even a single day was allowed to pass. "The wages of him that is hired shall not abide with thee all night until the morning."[2] But as no specific rules can entirely prevent the tendency of some people to accumulate and of others to lose, a redivision of the land was required every fifty years. This looks like Christian socialism carried to its utmost limit.

But the system was not permanently successful. As the nation began to forget God, the grasping tendency of human nature asserted itself more and more, till the rights

---

[1] Lev. xxiii. 22.   [2] Lev. xix. 13.

of the poor were again wholly ignored. Abstract law and justice must be illustrated and reinforced by the power of a *life*. The Lawgiver himself came to the earth in the person of Jesus Christ, to show that love and self-sacrifice afford the only foundation for the permanent welfare of human society.

In considering the dark problems of the world it must be remembered that a large share of its sufferings arise from "man's inhumanity to man." If the evils which grow directly or indirectly out of human selfishness and human greed could be eliminated, the residuum would be comparatively small. God himself cannot prevent these evils without interfering with man's free will, and hence with his education. But the laws and influences he has introduced for their amelioration are truly wonderful, and should inspire us with a profound sense of gratitude and reverence. Some of these laws have already been mentioned in the discussion of specific evils. A few more will now be mentioned.

A person falling is entirely unconscious during the descent, whether the distance be great or small. This is proved by the universal testimony of those who have passed through the experience.

There is no pain in death by drowning. Those who have been resuscitated describe the sensation as rather pleasurable than otherwise.

Wounds on a battle-field are rarely felt at the time. The excitement exalts the soldier above the consciousness of bodily injury.

The much-dreaded act or process of death, from whatever cause, is painless. The struggles which sometimes occur, though painful to witness, are not accompanied by suffering, as they do not usually begin till after the point of consciousness is past.

Human nature is endowed with a marvelous power of adaptation to a new environment. Emerson says: "We never find ourselves under novel conditions but they immediately seem to fit us like a garment." Bayard Taylor relates that when he once assumed the dress of a Bedouin and entered into the life of the children of the desert as an experiment, he was in a few days completely adapted to the new condition. His previous life seemed like a dream. The occasional receipt of letters from the outside world gave him a painful shock, as of something foreign to his nature.

Even when the new condition is one of disease—suffering from an incurable malady—the mysterious law of adaptation often works with singular power. There is something in the human heart which inspires, even under the severest trials, an instinctive belief in the divine goodness. "I cannot reconcile the thought of a loving God with the suffering of my mother" (from an incurable disease), was the remark of a friend. "What does she say about it?" "Oh, she does not complain. On the contrary, she is continually praising God for his goodness." And thus is it always. Grace for the ordeal is sure to be given to the trusting heart.

The subject of "God's ameliorations" should be considered in a volume rather than a chapter. With all our study and investigation we can never know a tithe of them, for they are a part of the divine care of each individual. Earth seems full of the "habitations of cruelty," yet there is one law of self-denial which extends to the lowest and meanest of mankind. *One half the human race is perpetually denying itself for the other half—parents for children.*

And, after the worst is said, as an offset to the vast sum of human suffering, witness the blessed tide of sympathy that grows out of it. The more sad and heart-rending the story, whether it be of a public calamity in our own land, a famine in India or China, or a tale of woe from the wretched slave-sheds of Africa, the more deeply the heart of the public is stirred, opening many fountains of tenderness in human souls. Among the evidences that the race is entering a stage of "higher education" is the fact that, through the telegraph, we are brought into daily contact with suffering humanity in all parts of the world. One of God's ways of increasing the sum of human sympathy is by increasing our knowledge of human sorrow.

In discussing this subject we must not overlook the fact that nations and communities, like individuals, have to be taught by discipline. A cholera scourge is sometimes necessary to lead a people to establish right sanitary conditions. A town is visited by an epidemic of diphtheria or typhoid fever. The devout speak of it as "a visitation of Divine Providence." The undevout laugh this idea to scorn, and point to hygienic laws persistently violated till the scourge came as inevitably as harvest follows seed-sowing. The Christian philosopher recognizes a truth on both sides. The evil was a result of natural laws, yet it was also overruled by the Divine Author of the laws and made to serve his purposes. To believe otherwise is to defy reason and banish hope. The sufferers were victims of sanitary neglect, but the Heavenly Father did not desert them. His infinite wisdom and love were employed to accomplish some foreseen result in every case.

CHAPTER XIX.

SHORT TALKS ON VITAL TOPICS.

ARE WE PILGRIMS OR TRAMPS?

If we regard this world as only a temporary abode, and are seeking "a better country, even a heavenly," we are pilgrims. If our thoughts and affections are centered upon the things of this life, we are tramps, and must eventually become inmates of God's everlasting poorhouse, wherever and whatever that may be. It is a question of aim and purpose and not of appearance. A pilgrim may be dusty, travel-stained, footsore, and anything but attractive in mien and guise. But he has a noble purpose and seeks a noble destiny.

The distinction between a pilgrim and a tramp does not depend upon outward appearances, nor upon the daily life and experience, even by the standards of this world. A tramp may manage to get a decent suit of clothes, and may even be willing to work an hour or two occasionally for a meal. The condemning fact is that he has no worthy object in view. He is a vagabond. He is a floating quantity with no definite relations to his fellow-men from which any good can possibly be derived. In other words, he is a tramp. Another may be more wretchedly dressed. He may not stop for an hour's work at any time, but press forward in the heat and dust, depending upon charity for his food, and sleeping wherever night overtakes him. But he is doing it only as a temporary expedient. He is sacrificing the present for something better in the future. He is a pilgrim, and is entitled to respect in spite of his poverty and dirt. Goldsmith traveled through Europe on foot, winning a scanty livelihood by playing the flute for the simple-minded peasants as he passed along. But he was not a tramp, for he had a worthy purpose. He was studying the customs of the country and the people.

The title of this discussion is not chosen with a sensational purpose, but with the hope of suggesting a profound lesson. It is exceedingly difficult not to be influenced strongly by outward conditions. If we have wealth, friends, the good opinion of the world, it is scarcely possible to realize that in God's sight we may be "poor and miserable and blind and naked"—in other words, tramps—instead of the fashionable pilgrims we appear to be. But it is not only by wealth and worldly prosperity that we may be deceived. Perhaps we pride ourselves upon the fact that we are not like our rich neighbor who thinks (as we suppose) that he is riding to heaven in his elegant carriage and expects to buy admission by his deeds of charity. The neighbor who seems to us so luxurious may be crushed by some hidden sorrow, and learning lessons of humility and submission to God's will which we do not suspect and which have no counterpart in our experience.

It is strange how little we are affected by our Lord's terrible warnings, which he took pains to repeat in so many forms. "Many shall seek to enter in and shall not be able." "The last shall be first, and the first last." The wheat and tares shall grow up together and cannot be known apart. "Let both grow together till the harvest." "The heart is deceitful above all things and desperately wicked." In view of these solemn words, is it not the part of wisdom to pause occasionally in the rush of life and ask the question, Am I a pilgrim or a tramp? Am I seeking to acquire the spirit, the habits of thought, and the customs of the Celestial Country, or am I, in spite of my professions, still adapting my life to the usages of this world with the desire to get all the comfort and luxury I can out of it? Do I praise with my lips the King of that country while I live in the indulgence of selfish propensities which he plainly says must be sacrificed? Am I resisting one set of temptations only to afford myself an excuse for yielding to another? A keen observer of human nature says, "People often exchange one sin for another and then think they have repented of the first one." Am I permitting Satan thus to deceive me? His wiles are endless. If he cannot lead us to do evil, he will tempt us to take pride in our goodness. "Yes," he says, "be good, be good. It is the very best plan you can adopt for making your way in the world." Thus through a subtle motive of selfishness he introduces the spirit of his evil kingdom and begins to weave a web which may at last entangle us fatally.

Against all such plausible arguments and considerations our Lord has placed the simple declaration, DENY SELF. This is a solid rock amid the dangerous currents that beset us on every side. It is the magnetic pole toward which our compass must ever turn as long as the journey of life shall last. Any thought of our "righteousness" which excludes the principle of self-denial is a dangerous delusion. There is a profound and suggestive truth in the remark of a modern author:[1] "*It is easier to deny the sinful self than to deny the righteous self.*"

Returning to our central thought of life as education, the pilgrim may be described as one who is striving to learn his lessons aright. He respects and loves the great Head of the university, and studies earnestly the various text-books of the institution—the written Word, the book of Nature, the laws of social life. The spiritual tramp has no interest in the school or its instructions. The pilgrim delights in lending a helping hand to his fellow-students. The tramp has no higher motive than his own gratification. The pilgrim desires to learn such lessons as will enable him after graduation to enter upon a life of eternal usefulness. The tramp seeks only to enjoy himself during his school-days, hoping by some means, he knows not what, to avoid the consequences which must result from violating the reasonable and beneficent laws of his Divine Teacher.

THE TWO DOCTRINAL HEMISPHERES: GOD'S SOVEREIGNTY AND MAN'S FREE AGENCY.

The discussions and controversies of religious doctrinaires have usually been carried to the most violent extreme when the distinctions which divided the contending parties were of the least practical value. In the former centuries the church was given up to bitter feuds over differences on small points of doctrine. Distinctions of expression were magnified beyond realities of meaning, and uncharitableness of spirit widely prevailed. Bitterness of theological strife passed into a proverb. It seems to modern thought the height of absurdity to divide the church of Christ into

[1] Mrs. Amelia E. Barr.

opposing factions over a subject that no human being can understand and no human judgment can decide.

Yet we of the present generation have little ground for self-complacency in this regard. Religious controversies and heresy trials are usually over questions that are of no more practical value than the above. They relate to subjects that are entirely beyond the possibility of human knowledge.

Calvinism and Arminianism—the doctrine of God's sovereignty and the doctrine of man's free agency—are two grand correlated truths. They are two hemispheres of which both are necessary to form a perfect whole. The time has arrived when this must be accepted as a basis of all intelligent discussion of religious subjects. The error of separating them belongs to the former days when keen intellects waged war over logical subtleties which had no practical bearing upon the realities of life.

Since we are now coming into a knowledge of fundamental truths, and of the universal laws which govern these truths, it is most important that the confusion of the old controversies should be entirely discarded. It is not a theory of metaphysics, but a simple fact, that God rules all things, and yet we are free and responsible moral agents. We act, and God rules in and through our actions. That we cannot understand the union of the two is not of the slightest consequence. We do not understand *anything* in this world. We are as ignorant of the nature of matter as of the nature of God. All difficulties grow out of our unwillingness to accept the truth without interposing our foolish questions. The doubts in our minds with regard to Divine Providence will disappear when we place ourselves upon this platform of belief: "God is a Sovereign Ruler and I am a responsible being. He tells me to 'go forward' and promises me strength and guidance. I will act according to my best ability and trust him for the rest."

The truth is that the most zealous of Arminians becomes a Calvinist the moment he begins to pray. He could not utter a word of prayer if he did not know in his heart that he is a responsible being. How unwise is it, therefore, to "take sides" and try to prove that Calvinism is true and Arminianism false, or that one doctrine is more important than the other. Both are true and hence both are essential. No truth can be omitted from God's plan, either in things material or things spiritual.

I do not forget—the Christian world should never forget—the grand service that was rendered by Calvin in emphasizing the truth of God's sovereignty at a time when it was especially needed. It gave a tone and vigor to religious faith and religious thought the value of which is beyond estimation. It afforded a granite foundation for the mass of theories and speculations which naturally grew out of the protesting period of the world's history. But the pendulum swung too far, as it always does in the actions and reactions of our limited human nature. It made God a despotic Ruler and man a helpless instrument in his hands.

Now we have gone to the opposite extreme, and while a controlling Providence is conceded in theory, the doctrine is so modified and explained away that it has lost nearly all its power over the hearts and lives of men. The daily paper which comes to me while writing these lines reports the address of a professor in one of the largest and most distinctively Christian colleges of America, which is typical of the method of treating the subject at the present time. The speaker says: "As believers in Providence, we hold that God preserves all things and controls all events. At the same time, our recognition of second causes involves a conviction that all events have their places in chains of natural antecedents and consequences, known or unknown." Let the reader judge for himself whether his belief in a *real* superintending and controlling Providence is strengthened or weakened by such dialectic statements. Do they not inevitably put God farther away and interpose a confusing medium between the Heavenly Father and his children?

This subject is one which cannot be treated metaphysically. It is the most real and vital and practical of questions for every human being. It affords the highest incentive and most powerful stimulus that can be presented to the mind. How to act with the intelligence, vigor, and effectiveness of absolute personal responsibility, and yet preserve a complete and restful faith in God's infinite care and coöperation—this is the problem for every Christian. Paul did not fear to grapple with it. He stated the proposition with its true antithesis in the following terms:

1. "Work out your own salvation with fear and trembling."

2. "It is God who worketh in you both to will and to do for his good pleasure."

WORKING WITH GOD.

It is God who works. Let us never for one moment forget this truth. It is God who is doing things. We are only instruments in his hand. "While it is true that God does not work without means, it is equally true that means cannot work without God."[1] Much is made in the old ecclesiastical writings of God's condescension. The term is a gigantic solecism. It is a thought which belongs wholly to our imperfect human state. The attitude of condescension is impossible with God. It is the essence of his nature to give. His giving is only limited by the capacity of any object, of any being, to receive. All who receive are to the extent of their receiving co-partners with him. On the other hand, their capacity for receiving will depend upon the degree of their giving. God cannot pour his life into a vessel that is already full. As we give, so we receive, and our labors are therefore only an expression of the life of Him whose province it is both "to will and to do." We cannot even make a fire without entering into the works of God. He stored the coal ages ago, or caused the forest to grow in later years, and the springing of the flame with its development of heat is by his direct act and power.

The proposition that God does all things introduces a perplexing thought. Does he act through the evil lives of wicked men? Yes. He acts through them, but not as he acts through good men who desire to work with him. Both are employed as instruments for doing his will, but one is an unwilling instrument—a resisting medium—while the other is a willing or consenting medium. Both are left in the free exercise of choice, but one, by choosing to be used, is placed by that choice in the current of Divine Providence. His work, therefore, brings him constantly into a closer union and sympathy with God, the Infinite Worker. The other, by choosing his own way, is led

[1] Rev. C. G. Hazard.

farther and farther away from God, although his acts are overruled and used for the accomplishment of the divine purpose.

Napoleon, a monster of selfish ambition, was employed as an instrument for rousing the nations of Europe from a state of stagnation and preparing them to perform their part in the stirring events of a new dispensation. He brought untold suffering to millions of people, but not a pang or a sorrow to one for whom God had not in his wise forethought prepared the experience and provided and arranged for all possible consequences.

But the Christian has nothing to do with the perplexing side of the question. He desires to give up his own will and take God's will in its place. This he can do in all the commonest duties of life, and in doing so his whole being is blessed. "A man is relieved and gay when he has put his heart into his work and done his best."[1] It is because Paul did this that his heart was so full of joy. The word "rejoice" is the key-note of his life and of his writings. "Rejoice in the Lord always: and again I say, Rejoice." "In everything give thanks."

Tolstoi has spoken wisely on the subject of "working with God." This brief discussion of the topic cannot be more fitly closed than with these words of his:

"God's work is within you. Approach it, and become, not a workman, but a son, and you will be a co-partner of God, who is infinite, and a sharer in his work. With God there is neither little nor great; there is only straight and crooked. Enter on the straight road in life, and you will be one with God, and your work will be neither great nor little; it will be God's work."

[1] Emerson.

WHAT IS CONVERSION?

In the new light which flows from a more scientific and rational consideration of certain fundamental truths, many Christians have been led to reconsider their views regarding the nature of conversion. They formerly supposed it to involve some kind of an intellectual conception of the "mediatorial sacrifice" of Christ, with a change of mental condition from a consciousness of guilt to a consciousness of forgiveness. Our Lord did not so explain it. He taught that it is the nature of his kingdom—the kingdom within—to come "without observation." He told Nicodemus that the new birth is like the wind, whose coming and going are beyond our knowledge. "So is every one that is born of the Spirit." Yet the former teachings concerning conversion have made it appear more like an earthquake. A deep conviction of sin followed by a more or less ecstatic sense of being forgiven—such has been the standard of the past. It is now giving way to a more scriptural and reasonable ideal. When relieved of all ecclesiastical and metaphysical subtleties, is not the following the true theory of conversion? *To be converted is to begin to follow Christ.*

He is the Way, the Truth, and the Life. To turn toward him is to turn away from selfishness and sin. To follow him is to follow good instead of evil. No one can truly follow him and keep his sayings without coming gradually into the possession of his spirit, that is to say, of the Divine Life.

How is it with those who from childhood have been trained in the "nurture and admonition of the Lord"? Must they also be converted?

The definition of conversion given above removes all the difficulties of the question. To be a Christian is to follow Christ. One who is already following Christ cannot *begin* to follow him. In this sense there is no room for conversion in the case of those who are taught to obey Christ from childhood. Dr. Bushnell disposed of that question fully and finally in his epoch-making volume "Christian Nurture." He says: "There could not be a worse or more baleful implication given to a child than that he is to reject God and all holy principle till he has come to a mature age. What authority have you from Scriptures to tell your child, or by any sign to show him, that you do not expect him truly to love and obey God till after he has spent whole years in hatred and wrong? Perhaps you do not give your child to expect that he is to grow up in sin; you only expect that he will yourself. That is scarcely better, for that which is your expectation will surely be his, and, what is more, any attempt to maintain a discipline at war with your own secret expectations will only make a hollow and worthless figment of that which should be an open, earnest reality. You will never practically aim at what you practically despair of, and if you do not practically aim to unite your child to God you will aim at something less; that is, something unchristian, wrong, sinful.

"'But my child is a sinner,' you will say, 'and how can I expect him to begin a right life until God gives him a new heart?' This is the common way of speaking, and I state the objection in its own phraseology, that it may recognize itself. Who, then, has told you that a child cannot have the new heart of which you speak? Whence do you learn that if you live the life of Christ before the child and with him, the law of the Spirit of Life may not be such as to include and quicken him also? And why should it be thought incredible that there should be some really good principle awakened in the mind of a child? For this is all that is implied in a Christian state. The Christian is one who has simply *begun* to love what is good for its own sake, and why should it be thought impossible for a child to have this love begotten in him? Take any scheme of depravity you please, there is yet nothing in it to forbid the possibility that a child should be led, in his first moral act, to cleave unto what is good and right any more in the first than in his twentieth year. He is, in that case, only a child converted to good, leading a mixed life as all Christians do. The good in him goes into combat with the evil and holds a qualified sovereignty. And why may not this internal conflict of goodness cover the whole life from its dawn, as well as any part of it? And what more appropriate to the doctrine of spiritual influence itself than to believe that as the Spirit of Jehovah fills all the worlds of matter, and holds a presence of power and government in all objects, so all human souls, the infantile as well as the adult, have a nurture of the Spirit appropriate to their age and wants? What opinion is more essentially monstrous, in fact, than that which regards the Holy Spirit as having no agency in the immature souls of children who are growing up, helpless and unconscious, into the perils of time?"

These questions carry their own answer, and they embody a line of argument which is unassailable. The strange misconception by Nicodemus of our Lord's figure of speech has affected all the theology of the past. While pitying his stupidity in giving such a mechanical interpretation to the figure, yet the notions regarding spiritual birth have been strongly colored by it. Nicodemus supposed it to be an actual physical birth. Many Christians have supposed it to be *like* the physical birth in its suddenness and its cataclysmal character. The Lord's own interpretation is that it is like the mysterious movement of the air. Paul's conversion has been regarded as typical, and so it is, in the truest sense. His conversion did not consist in his heavenly vision, nor in his falling to the ground, nor in his subsequent blindness. His new life began with the question, "Lord, what wilt thou have me to do?" And so must it be with every child of the race. Eternal life begins at the moment when "the good in him goes into combat with the evil." If that, through the wise guidance of parents, has begun in early childhood, it has only to be continued, or perhaps resumed, in later years. To follow Christ is always safe and always saving.

THE KINGDOM WITHIN.

No more pregnant truth has been uttered in this generation than that expressed by Professor John Fiske concerning the history of evolution. His thought is this. "There is a stage in the evolutionary process when man's development ceases to be physical and becomes psychical; the growth of the body ends and the growth of the soul begins." This is an epic poem in a sentence. It marks the end of the supposed antagonism between science and religion. It announces an eternal marriage of the two—a union which will grow more complete and mutually helpful in all time to come. It is a response of the nineteenth century to the first, when the Lord of the universe heralded the psychical era by stating its fundamental law, "The kingdom of God is within you."

When this spiritual axiom is received—practically and vitally received—by any individual, it exercises a transforming influence upon his life. Old things pass away. All things become new. There are many Christians who do not have a full realization of this truth. The mechanical theory of salvation, with its substitution of another's righteousness, is not favorable to it. Let it be repeated a thousand times, if necessary, that the substitution theory was not derived and is not derivable from the teachings of Christ. It was an outgrowth of medieval ecclesiasticism, a crystallization of monarchical ideas, supported by isolated texts from the Scriptures. The Saviour's instructions were wholly addressed to the inner life. They were based upon a mystical union of the soul with God, "as the branch is joined to the vine." No process but growth is conceivable in connection with his instructions and the life they enjoin. To deny self, to be meek, to be pure in heart, to trust God's providence—all that he taught was of the nature of seed, to be received into the heart, to be expressed in the life, to bear fruit, to cause such a going forth of love to our fellow-men that we should be united to them even as he and the Father were united. All God's dealings with us have reference to the inner, spiritual kingdom. Material things and earthly experiences have no purpose but to serve the interests of that kingdom. This is the meaning of the injunction that while we are *in* the world we are not to be *of* it, that we are to make friends of the mammon of unrighteousness, and many others of the same nature. He who cultivates the inner life, the life of the spirit, is helping to build heaven. This is the descent of the New Jerusalem spoken of in the Apocalypse.

Many Christian people are troubled because the boundary line between the church and the world seems less sharply defined than formerly. This comes mostly from a modification of views regarding certain external forms of social life. In reality, the distinction is deeper than it has been in the past, because the emphasis of Christian life is being placed where it belongs—on the character rather than on the renunciation of certain so-called worldly pleasures. In other words, the test is now positive instead of negative. The fruits of the Spirit as described by the sacred Scriptures are the inward graces which place the soul in a right attitude toward God and our fellow-men. Here is the heavenly catalogue: "Love, joy, peace, longsuffering, kindness, goodness, faithfulness, meekness, temperance." Can we say there is not a strong line of demarkation between those who bear such fruit and those who do not?

The new age is a psychical age. It is an era in which the " kingdom within" will be understood for what it is—the *only* kingdom. There is no other. The material universe is merely an accessory; a temporary expedient; a birthplace for the soul; a stairway by which it may rise to its eternal abiding-place in the unseen world.

"The spiritual is the beginning and the end. The material is a little unknown something that comes between."

THE STUPIDITY OF INGRATITUDE.

Every human being desires to be happy. Even the philosopher who insists that self-denial is better than self-indulgence, and nobility of character better than happiness, is in reality arguing for a deeper and more permanent kind of happiness. Such being the universal aim, what must be thought of the universal tendency to indulge a habit of mind which renders happiness next to impossible?

In a world so full of imperfections and limitations, there can be but one method of securing the contentment which is the basis of all true happiness. Each person must study his own condition and circumstances in order to ascertain the sum of his blessings as compared with his disadvantages. Yet this is precisely what we usually fail to do. We leave our blessings uncounted and permit ourselves to be annoyed and made unhappy by every vexation or petty trial that may chance to beset us. What better title can be given to this habit than to characterize it as the stupidity of ingratitude? The loss of sight is a dire misfortune. Is not, then, its daily preservation an occasion for daily gratitude? Yet how little do we feel, and how rarely do we express, any sense of gratitude for the perpetual miracle of our bodily health. Our "common mercies" may not be consciously despised, but they awaken in our hearts but a slight degree of conscious appreciation.

In order to stir our minds to a proper sense of shame, let us record a partial list of the blessings we so ungratefully and stupidly permit to be overshadowed by the trifling vexations of daily life.

1. Souls made in the image of God with a capacity for eternal growth and eternal happiness.

2. Bodies which are marvelously fitted to serve us as long as we need them.

3. Faculties or senses which enable us to enjoy all that is good and beautiful in the physical universe.[1]

---

[1] " Man stands in the midst of the universe, and all things gravitate toward him, all things seek to serve him, and the Lord has given him the capacity to receive service from all. He has made him an embodied want, that he might

4. Homes filled with appliances for comfort and luxury which we inherit from the inventive genius of man as it has been exercised during all the ages of the past. The kings and nobles of former times knew nothing of many luxuries that now belong to the common people.

have the blessedness of supplying his wants, and might bless man in receiving the supply. Man is an organized vessel, and he can receive from the lowest and the highest, from the rock and from the Lord. He has a cup for every good and truth—for water, for wine, for oil, for bread. Man is an exquisitely delicate sensorium capable of being affected by all contacts. The human body is the brain of the earth, and there are fibers running from it to every rock and fluid and gas and plant and animal, and by these nervous fibers it gains a knowledge of every motion and change of state, so that a blade of grass cannot grow, or a leaf change its quality, or a flower exhale its fragrance, or a bird sing in the forest, but man will know it, so intimately is he conjoined to the material world. Indeed, the universe is only a larger body for the soul.

"The Lord seeks us through every channel. He offers himself in every gift; seeks to awaken and call all the powers he has given us into play, that he may flow in and conjoin us more intimately to himself. He has made it necessary for us to take stated supplies of food and given us a relish for it; and he has made the sea a storehouse and the earth a granary filled with the richest and most varied abundance, not only to supply our natural wants and to gratify a natural appetite, but that we might taste the sweetness of that loving care which made the provision. He has formed us to love variety, and he has created no two things alike, that he might minister to this love and at the same time reveal to us the exhaustless riches of his bounty. Beauty delights us, and he has filled the world with it; molded stones and shells and flowers and fruits and animals into the most graceful, delicate, and lovely forms, that he might lead us to the supreme beauty through the natural delight. So through every sense he gives us natural delights, and through these natural delights he seeks to give us spiritual delights, and through these to conjoin us to himself. Take a pebble, a rose, a grain of wheat, a ray of light, or a tone of music, and examine it carefully in the light of spiritual truth, and you will discover fine, delicate filaments running through it, entering the eye, or ear, or touch, or taste, and winding themselves into the inmost recesses of your being. Take the thread into your hand, and let your thoughts and affections follow the clew, and it will lead them through many winding ways, perhaps, but directly, according to true order, to the bosom of infinite love."—REV. CHAUNCEY GILES.

5. The Bible in every home, and the noblest thoughts of all ages placed within our reach by the miracle of the printing-press.

6. Society organized for our protection, leaving us free to go and come as we please, with no fear of the evil-minded, affording the privilege of peaceable worship.

7. The mightiest forces of nature subdued to our will and brought into our service. Time and space annihilated for our benefit.

8. News from every part of the world served to us with our morning meal.

9. Comfortable clothing for our bodies, and food sufficient for the day's need.

10. Great educational advantages for ourselves and our children.

11. Friends and sympathy according to our capacity to appreciate the one and to deserve the other.

12. The promise of a perfect and everlasting life after we are through with this imperfect and temporary existence.

13. To remove all ground for discouragement and dissatisfaction in a world which our Heavenly Father knows to be full of difficulties, hindrances, and temptations, he has given his solemn word and promise that whatever may happen to us will be overruled for good. He engages to bear all the responsibility and all the care, leaving us free-handed and free-hearted for our work.

In contrast with this list of blessings, how amazing is the pettiness, the childishness of our daily troubles. They are too puerile to enumerate, and yet we permit them to engross nearly all our thoughts and to give a somber coloring to our lives. We even allow them to write themselves upon our faces. How rarely do we meet a bright, sunny countenance, expressing a grateful enjoyment of God's boundless gifts! Every one, or, at least, every Christian, will acknowledge ingratitude to be a sin. Perhaps it will serve as a healthful stimulus to be reminded that it is also idiotically stupid. We wish to be happy, yet neglect the only means that can possibly produce happiness. We long to have our days filled with sunshine, yet, by forgetting our Father's promises, we permit a dark cloud of cares, anxieties, and gloomy forebodings to gather about us and exclude the heavenly rays. No plant can grow without proper soil for its nourishment; yet we expect the delicate flower of happiness to flourish in our hearts without providing the only nutriment on which it can subsist—a grateful appreciation of our blessings, and a loving acknowledgment of our Father's wisdom and goodness in providing them.

The folly of ingratitude to God is illustrated by the natural consequences of ingratitude among men. When people are unappreciative and exacting, how soon we grow weary of ministering to them. Hence the benefits they receive from their fellows grow continually less. It is true that God's love is not imperfect like ours. It is infinite, and his patience is untiring. Yet his gifts and blessings to the children of men are limited by an inexorable law. It is a part of his very being to give, but he cannot give to those who will not receive. Ingratitude is inevitably narrowing. It so closes the absorbents of the soul, if we may so express it, that even the benign influence of the Heavenly Father cannot enter with its life-giving power. Ingratitude begins by limiting God's gifts, and ends by excluding them altogether. It thus, if carried to its extreme result, ends in eternal death by rejecting the source of life.

WHAT MUST THE CHRISTIAN DO TO BE SAVED?

"Nothing," is perhaps the first thought of a Christian reader. "I *am* saved, by my faith in the Lord Jesus Christ. My work in the future is not to secure salvation, which is already mine, but to grow in grace and in the knowledge and power of God."

This is true, and yet it is not all the truth. It is a half-truth which misleads many souls. It disappears in the clear light of our Saviour's instructions when rightly understood. All that he taught during his entire ministry may be summed up in two words, "life" and "growth." "I came that they might have *life*, and that they might have it more abundantly." "Consider the lilies of the field how they *grow*." Not one word did he utter which, when rightly understood, will not be found to reinforce the theory of growth in the divine life which he came to impart. Salvation means "health," and there can be no spiritual health without spiritual growth.

What must the sinner do to be saved? He must be born from above. He must join himself by faith to the one only Source of life.

What must the Christian do to be saved? He must receive and appropriate that life day by day, and hour by hour, and bring forth the fruits of the Christ-life in him. "By their fruits ye shall know them."

What must the branch do to be saved? It must be vitally joined to the vine. It must receive, assimilate, and utilize the life-blood of the parent stock. There is but one evidence that the branch has properly fulfilled this duty, and that evidence is fruit. Leaves, however abundant, do not constitute evidence. Fruit, and fruit alone, is proof that the branch is doing the will of the vine.

This is the Lord's own lesson and illustration. The world has been deprived of its beauty and power by the artificial discriminations of a scholastic and polemical age. The naturalness and force of the figure have been destroyed, and hence its value and helpfulness as a medium for conveying a vital truth has been seriously impaired.

If the illustration means anything, it cannot mean less than this: *A Christian is only a Christian so far as he is a Christian;* that is, so far as he translates Christian principles into Christian living. This is not the standard of theological dogma, with its theory of a magical transformation. The transformation from death to life *is* magical, but no more so in the spiritual birth of a human soul than in the germination of a grain of wheat. The law of growth belongs as much to the Christian after his birth as to the grain of wheat after its germination, or as the body of a child after its birth into the world.

All the forces of nature unite to aid the growth of a plant or tree. The earth, the sunshine, the rain, the air— all contribute to its life, and do their utmost to carry it on to the fulfilment of its destiny. So do all the providences of God help to build the eternal life of the Christian. Instead of having nothing to do for his salvation because he is a Christian, he has everything to do for that one distinct reason. He must establish and confirm the germ of Christianity in his soul. He must grow in every principle and truth taught by his Lord and Master. He must become an embodied Sermon on the Mount. Paul speaks of it as " making our calling and election sure." Peter says, " As he which called you is holy, be ye yourselves also holy in all manner of living."

The law of growth in salvation is thus described by Professor Drummond: " Religion is the simplest thing in the world. Things here go on not by caprice, but by law—law absolutely simple, absolutely unerring. It is the everlasting lesson of science: law is sure and inevitable. Let us get into the Christian life a little science. Nature and the eternal truths of God are older than religion, and they pervade religion. Our common every-day lives are the means God employs to build up our Christian lives. A farm or an office are not places to make crops or money, but men. All the little things about our daily toil are the framework and scaffolding of our spiritual life."

HEAVENLY CONVERSATION.

Christian evolution opens a new world of suggestion to every thoughtful mind. It revolutionizes social life by revolutionizing all our views of life. Heretofore our earthly existence has been regarded as a mere fragment—the brief and uncertain tenancy of a small planet in the solar system. Another existence elsewhere was anticipated with various shades of hope and fear, but in its nature and essence it was entirely separate and distinct from this. Human thought is now transfigured, lifted out of itself by the truth which follows as a necessary corollary from the doctrine of an immanent God.

Life is one and continuous. Eternal life is a conscious life in God. It belongs as truly on one side of death as the other. The present and future worlds represent differences of quantity rather than of quality. To have the conversation in heaven therefore does not necessarily mean talk about a place, but a discussion of the principles which prevail there. The true rendering of the sentence is " Our *citizenship* is in heaven." This makes the case even more clear. Our interest is identical with our citizenship. If we visit a foreign country for a temporary purpose, retaining the citizenship of our native land, the latter still remains the center of our interest and affection. Nothing gives us more pleasure than to meet our fellow-countrymen and talk with them of the beloved home-land and all that belongs to it, and especially of the principles it represents.

Heaven is a place where God is all in all, and where everything that is seen, heard, or enjoyed is accepted as an expression of his love, wisdom, and goodness. Heavenly conversation in this world is that which is based upon a similar recognition. If in our discussions we speak of God as the Source or Author of all that exists here, and of all that transpires, our intercourse will be allied to that of the angels. In this line of thought there is no temptation to unconscious hypocrisy. In truth, it is scientific, and is rapidly coming to be so regarded. We cannot even speak of a remarkable invention without recognizing God as the Creator of the genius from which it sprang. In the deepest analysis it must be perceived that he is in reality the author of the invention itself. Charles Talbot Porter says: " Man cannot create thought any more than he can create matter. Both must come from God." Goethe says: " All the thinking in the world does not bring us thoughts. One must be right by nature, so that good thoughts may come before us like free children of God and cry, ' Here we are.' "

Heavenly conversation is to the last degree elevating and ennobling. It lifts the thoughts above all pettiness. It avoids sectarianism, and banishes unworthy social distinctions. The poor and unlearned man, as truly as the rich and wise, can see God in all things. It affords a bond of sympathy between the wise and the simple. If the man of learning will speak of God's marvels in nature, in science, or in life, it will not sound pedantic, and the ignorant will listen with pleasure and without a painful consciousness of inferior culture.

The thought of an immanent God gives dignity to the most commonplace subjects. As bees in gathering honey fertilize the flowers, so shall we in seeking to find God in all things fructify our own minds and the minds of others, creating new thoughts and inspiring a nobler range of sentiment. Even a common pebble will call forth reverential feelings if we realize that the attraction which holds it in form is a direct exercise of God's power. The objects of nature, the experiences of daily life, business, the welfare of the community, the cabled tidings from other lands, in truth, all subjects that are worth talking about, may be brought within the category of heavenly conversation by a simple recognition of the truth that God is and must be in all things.

> This one theme: that whate'er be the fate that has hurt us or joyed,
> Whatever the face that is turned to us out of the void,
> Be it cursing or blessing, or night or the light of the sun,
> Be it ill, be it good, be it life, be it death, it is ONE:
> One thought, and one law, and one awful and infinite power,
> In atom, in world, in the bursting of fruit and of flower,
> The laughter of children, and roar of the lion untamed,
> And the stars in their courses—one Name that can never be named.[1]

[1] Richard Watson Gilder.

ATMOSPHERIC RELIGION, OR SPIRITUAL RADIATION.

One of the most successful lawyers in New York City was asked to tell the secret of his success. He replied: "When I began to practise in the courts I adopted the expedient of trying to create an atmosphere whenever I appeared in public. I would come into the court-room a little late. I would then arrange my books and papers with a certain air as if much depended upon their being at hand at exactly the right moment. By these and many other little devices I succeeded in giving the impression that I was a lawyer with serious and important ideas in my head, and one who was pretty certain to bring something to pass. My early success undoubtedly arose from my creating such an impression."

There is a profound lesson in this for the Christian. Here is a worldly man, who, with purely selfish and ambitious motives, is able to surround himself by an atmosphere which shapes the opinions of all with whom he comes in contact. If this can be done for self-aggrandizement, it can be done equally for the benefit of others. It is true that we create an atmosphere unconsciously, but it is also true that we can do much to modify this unconscious influence. We all know how much we are influenced by the sphere of those about us. A casual meeting with a bright and genial nature will give us pleasant feelings for an entire day, while a momentary contact with one of the opposite kind will leave a sting that it is hard to get rid of.

Nothing helps so much to create in the soul what may be called spiritual radiation as a firmly established belief in Divine Providence. Doubtless every true Christian desires to give out a helpful influence as he goes through life, but we are apt to forget that our troubles and trials afford a golden opportunity to inspire and encourage others. Nothing makes so strong an impression upon us as to see bravery and cheerfulness under severe discipline. We admire it above all things. We commend it without stint. Yet when our turn comes to illustrate the virtue we flinch and falter. Our smiles vanish. Our cheerful words are wanting. The scores of centuries since Jacob's time have taught us nothing. The marvels of providential history which he who runs may read do not prevent us from echoing the patriarch's querulous plaint, "All these things are against me."

Our chief mistake is in failing to realize that the unconscious outgiving of our lives can be consciously cultivated. We do not wish to go about with a ready-made smile, nor to strive by a vacuous amiability to make others happy, and so we give up altogether, thinking our unconscious influence must take care of itself. This is a great error. To cultivate a cheerful spirit is to cultivate a cheerful atmosphere. We may conceal our thoughts, but we cannot conceal our souls. The radiation of our inward being is inevitable. It may, therefore, in fact it imperatively should, be an incentive to cultivate faith, courage, a hopeful way of looking at things—in a word, all the spiritual gifts and graces—because in doing so we are helping others as well as ourselves.

This is what is meant when we are urged to become living epistles, known and read of all men. Epistles we are, and read we will be, in spite of ourselves. Who would not wish to be a constant love-letter from God to the world? This is exactly what Christ wants us to be, and what he came to show us how to be. He was a perfect exponent and illustration of atmospheric religion, of spiritual radiation.

SPIRITUAL LAW IN THE NATURAL WORLD.

Occasionally a book appears which either makes or marks a new era in the intellectual history of the race. Professor Drummond's "Natural Law in the Spiritual World" may be fairly classed among such works. It marked, and helped in some degree to create, an epoch in the method of presenting religious truth. The title alone was sufficient to indicate a novel field of investigation. It started a new train of thought in every reflecting mind. Yet it is a singular fact that the line of reasoning suggested by the title, if followed out to logical conclusions, shows the true order of cause and effect to be just the opposite, and requires a reversal of the terms. To be accurate we should speak of "Spiritual Law in the Natural World."

This is not said in criticism of Professor Drummond's title, which simply expresses his point of view—that of one standing upon the earth and looking upward. He does not fail to recognize the truth that "the first in the field was the spiritual world." He distinctly states that God's plan and order must be to "project the higher laws downward so that the Natural World would become an incarnation, a visible representation, a working model of the spiritual." Again he says: "The visible is the ladder up to the invisible; the temporal is but the scaffolding of the eternal."

All this being true, it is evident that a change of standpoint from the material world to the spiritual must afford us many helpful suggestions. We are already so prepossessed by a belief in the reality of matter that our only hope of escaping from its dominion is to transfer our thoughts to the opposite end of the line and study the various phenomena of nature and of life from the spiritual side. We must recognize the spiritual world as the world of causes, and the natural world as the world of effects or results. If we place ourselves in imagination beyond the veil of the unseen, we range our thoughts on the side of causation. We can then follow the Divine Power in its various forms of manifestation or ultimation. We see it acting upon matter and holding it in place by the power which is known in human language as attraction. We see it acting upon the seed in the soil, causing it to germinate, and afterward supplying the principle of life till the plant or tree is grown. We see it enter the bud in early spring, setting the sap in motion and continuing its creative influence till the perfect leaf or flower is produced. We see it begin its mysterious work upon an egg, or the ovary of an animal, and in due time the living creature is given to the world. In the realm of moral things we see it acting upon men's hearts and moving them as strongly toward that which is good and true and lovely as can be done without interfering with their freedom.

It is a predominating characteristic of the present age that the spiritual is beginning to be recognized as the only real, and that there are no laws in the universe but spiritual laws. Many as yet see this truth very imperfectly. Like him whose eyes were partially healed, they see "men as trees walking." They fear that faith in the supernatural is being driven out of the world because they fail to recognize the growth of a deeper truth in human thought—namely, the supernaturalness of the natural. "Christ is being robbed of his divinity," they cry in real distress, which is born of loyalty to their Master. "They have taken away my Lord, and I know not where they have laid him."

There is no ground for fear, but rather cause for infinite rejoicing. The bold and reverent thinkers of to-day are but penetrating the theological fog and mist which arose during the long era of scholastic speculation. They are only revealing truths which have been concealed or obscured. In showing the "reign of law" they are breaking the last bonds of superstition which turned the divinely simple teachings of Jesus into a complex system. Thousands of volumes have been written to prove and establish a "theory" of the atonement when there is nothing of theory involved in it. Jesus, a revealer and interpreter of the Heavenly Father's love, came "to seek and to save that which was lost." A little child can understand it. And when he is old enough to understand the "law of sacrifice" which his mother manifested in her care of him, surrendering her entire being for his welfare, going to death for it if necessary, he can also comprehend the same law in the life and death of his Redeemer.

THE LORD JESUS CHRIST AS AN EVOLUTIONIST.

When a new truth is planted in the world it must take root in whatever soil it finds. The instructions of Christ were all based upon the principle of evolution or growth. They involved the idea of growth; but the world was not prepared to understand the principle. Human knowledge was crude and undeveloped. The laws of nature, God's methods of operation in the universe, were utterly unknown. They were not even remotely suspected by the greatest minds. It is not merely an aptly turned phrase, but an interesting statement of fact, that " until Bacon's time educated people did not think of nature, but of what Aristotle said about nature."

The result was natural and inevitable. During the first century, while Christian believers were still under the direct power of that wonderful Life, they were moved and largely controlled by a principle which they did not understand. After that time the tendencies of human nature began to assert themselves. Men sought, and found, mechanical or artificial methods of explaining the deep fundamental principles of love and life. They made the vital mistake of putting formulations of truth above the fruits of a loving life, the results of which are to be seen in the melancholy history of the succeeding centuries.

But truth cannot be destroyed. All the way along there were simple hearts to receive and earnest lives to express the law of love as proclaimed by the Saviour of the world. It was like a smoldering fire breaking out here and there in spite of all efforts to quench it. At different epochs men were raised up to bear new witness to the old and eternal truth. Holy men and women like John Tauler, Jacob Boehme, Fénelon, and Madame Guyon were evolved at various stages of the history to guide and inspire the faithful representatives of a Gospel of Love.

Yet the law of evolution in spiritual things could not be understood till its methods in the material world were revealed and to some extent comprehended. This educational process is now sufficiently advanced to permit an intelligent study of our Lord's instructions in the light of the evolutionary method. This method is, in fact, nothing but the ways of an "immanent God" in the physical universe and in the realm of moral and spiritual realities. The acknowledgment of the devout scientist that what we call gravitation is a direct act of the Creator holding the heavenly orbs in their places—the Divine Will acting through matter—is a helpful commentary on the Lord's statement that his followers must be joined to him as the branch is joined to the vine. They are two sides of one and the same truth, namely, that there is no power or life in the universe but the divine power and the divine life. The divine power constructs the heavenly bodies and holds them in their places; the divine life must be consciously received and appropriated as the branch receives and appropriates the life-blood of the vine.

Jesus Christ is often spoken of as a reformer, but it is only within a very few years that it has begun to dawn upon the world that he was a *model* reformer. He laid the foundation for the methods of regenerating society which we regard as new and peculiar to this progressive age. In the words "Except ye become as little children ye cannot enter the kingdom of heaven" are found the warranty for the kindergarten. When he said, "If any man will do God's will he shall know of the doctrine," he announced the educational law, "We learn to do by doing." It was the statement of a universal principle. If we wish to know the doctrine or truth concerning wood or iron, we must work according to its laws, i.e., do its will. This is the basis of the recent enlargement of the plan for human culture known as industrial education. Much is made in these days of ethical culture, but it is impossible to proceed on that line without practically following the instructions given in the Sermon on the Mount. And all societies banding men together to do Christ's will are but developments of his original plan for the church. Thus it appears upon a careful analysis that the germ of every modern movement or effort for the elevation of humanity is to be found in Christ's words. And beneath every other law is the universal law of life, "Do unto others as ye would that they should do unto you."

CHAPTER XX.

EVOLUTION AND THE CHRISTIAN DOCTRINES.

WHEN Newton announced the theory of gravitation the Christian world was filled with alarm. The cause of religion seemed to be imperiled by the substitution of a law or force for the direct act of the Almighty. Two centuries later a similar alarm is created by the theory of evolution. Indeed, it has been distinctly claimed by eminent materialists that the law of development dismisses " supernaturalism " to the limbo of exploded superstitions. The boast was premature. A deeper scrutiny and a more comprehensive study and application of its own laws reveals the truth that evolution, like gravitation, instead of banishing God from the universe, only leads to a more profound knowledge, in fact, to the only true knowledge, of his methods in the universe. .

This is now widely conceded by the most advanced men of science. Yet while freely acknowledging that Theism is not displaced by the evolutionary theory, it is supposed to be beyond dispute that no room is found in that theory for the doctrines of the Christian system, such as the fall of man, human depravity, foreordination, and the like.

A thorough and comprehensive study of the subject shows that this idea, also, is an error. Evolution carries its transforming power into the realm of the moral and spiritual as truly as into the physical. Indeed, its mission in that realm is as much more important than in the other as the spiritual is higher than the physical. It comes upon the field just at the right moment, as God's instruments always do. It comes at this particular juncture, when the sudden emancipation of the public mind from human traditions is in danger of sending vast numbers of intelligent people out into the desolate regions of infidelity or agnosticism. To ascribe unjust and unreasonable conduct to God and then claim that he is not amenable to human ideas of justice will not satisfy any thoughtful or discriminating mind. The prevailing sentiment is expressed by George MacDonald's definition of justice as "fair play." The world must be made to see that God's dealings are infinitely wise and good, being founded upon the same laws that he has implanted in the nature of man, who was created in his image.

If the progress of spiritual truth required the renunciation of all former statements of doctrine, there would be no help for it. The truth must have its way, and none can hinder it. But fortunately this sweeping process is not necessary. Copernicus did not banish the sun from the heavens; he only showed us our true relation to it. It is thus with the fundamental doctrines of the Christian religion. We are not forced to the unpleasant conclusion that our ancestors were given up for centuries to mere childish delusions. There was a basis for the various doctrines, although it was imperfectly understood. As the basis was not clear, it followed as an inevitable consequence that the theological formulations were correspondingly inadequate. The theory of the divine immanence as expressed in evolution gives an eternal foundation for all religious truth, and a perfect logical consistency to the truth itself. This can best be shown by treating specifically of the various doctrines. A very brief consideration will first be given to the divine fountain of truth.

THE BIBLE.

The Bible has stood unmoved through all the mutations of human history because it embodies eternal truth. It has often seemed to be in peril, and its doom has been pronounced times without number. The dangers which appeared to threaten it have always proved to be merely a change of view which was necessitated by the growth of knowledge among men.

If the theory of evolution is correct, and if the Bible is a divine book, there can never be a conflict between the two. There is no such conflict. Truth never opposes truth. It is a miracle beyond all miracles that the Bible was adapted in its language to the former conditions of human ignorance, and yet proves to be a sufficient expression of the truth for man in his highest development. The law of evolution is plainly evident in its pages. There is a steadily growing consensus of opinion among Bible students that revelation has been progressive. It progressed from its first adaptation to a people who believed in many gods to the fundamental revelation of God as One. It progressed from a standard of Divine Providence limited to this world to one which included the future life. It progressed from injunctions to external morality to the higher law which requires purity of motive as well as of act.

It is a great misfortune that we are not permitted to read the Bible with our own unaided vision. We all look at it through colored glasses. Human definitions and systems stand between us and the Word. We almost unavoidably read from it what has been read into it by other minds than our own. A great and overshadowing error, which has come to us as an unfortunate heredity from the heated polemics of the past and from a stage of human development when such an idea was natural and perhaps inevitable, is that our Heavenly Father is a God of wrath. There is one theory, and only one, which will save the Bible from the human vagaries which continually gather around it: it must be treated as a purely spiritual book, requiring a spiritual interpretation of its contents in order to gain a full and correct knowledge of their meaning. The Bible is to be regarded as a spiritual book for the following reasons:

1. Because God, its author, is a spirit.
2. Because we for whom it is written are spirits.
3. Our immortal life is not to be spent in a material world, but in a spiritual world.
4. As God is a spirit, his thoughts must be spiritual.
5. As we are spiritual beings, the thoughts God addresses to us must be intended to reach and affect our spiritual natures. Such of his words as concern material things must be only an adaptation to our material condition and environment, with a spiritual meaning and purpose beneath the natural expression.

If we accept the Bible as a spiritual book we will study it solely for spiritual instruction. The question of the authorship of certain of its books is important as a matter of historical interest, but is not vital to the spiritual growth of the Christian. We shall be unmoved by all discussions of the chronology of the Pentateuch, the staying of the sun upon Gibeon, or the experience of Jonah with the whale. We shall seek to derive spiritual lessons from all its infinitely varied aspects of the truth. As the history of the children of Israel is now regarded as a picture or an epitome of the individual life of a Christian, so we will endeavor to apply all scriptural instructions profitably for our own growth in grace. If the condemnatory Psalms are read with the idea that our sins are the enemies spoken of, which we are bound to struggle against, to overcome, to exterminate, a new and inspiring meaning will be given to the passages which have heretofore been the hardest to understand. The sentence "Precious in the sight of the Lord is the death of his saints" is full of comfort in its most obvious signification, yet what an added depth is given to the meaning when we carry the thought into the realm of spiritual life and apply it to the death of self, the gradual overcoming of the self principle in our daily lives.

If, as we now believe, God speaks of spiritual things through the revelations of nature, how can we do otherwise than conclude that there are deeper spiritual truths in the Bible than are always to be seen in the first reading of the literal text?

EVOLUTION AND THE FALL.

The theory of man's fall, as generally accepted by the Christian bodies, appears on the surface to be totally at variance with the laws of evolution. The former describes the progress of the race as downward, while the latter shows it to be upward. The antagonism is only in appearance. Because the Bible speaks of man as made in the image of God it has been assumed that this image was perfect and in its highest development at the outset. This is a necessary corollary of the theory of an instantaneous creation, which teaches that all things were called into complete and perfectly organized existence by a word of command.

Evolution does not fail, even at this critical point. It involves a fall as well as a rising. The nature of the fall is indicated by the history of the individual man. The most valuable generalization that ever has or ever can be deduced from the revelations of science is that the individual is an epitome of the race. This is true, first, of his physical being. "Animals start in the womb as a single cell. As the human embryo grows it becomes like a fish, a reptile, a mammal, and finally takes the human form. It thus passes through the series of the ramified classification of animals, the kingdom, subkingdom, class, order, family, genus, and species."[1]

The parallelism is not merely a general resemblance, but extends to the smallest details. For instance, the earliest and simplest organisms have no organ of vision whatever. As the type rises and the organism becomes more complex, a small black spot appears where the eye is afterward to be formed. Still later the rudiments of nerves are to be seen behind the spot, which develop till the more highly organized animal is doubtless conscious of a glimmering of light. This process continues as the type ascends till the miracle of the eye is complete. If for any reason the nerves are not called into exercise, the eye begins to deteriorate, the creative process is reversed, till at last only the black spot remains, as may be seen in the fish of the Mammoth Cave.

[1] Rev. James McCosh, D.D.

In the human fœtus the eye passes through or reproduces the entire history of the visual mechanism in the evolution of the animal kingdom. There is first a black spot, then the rudiments of nerves, and finally, at birth, the perfect organ of vision.

"Man's body," says a recent writer, "contains the elements of all knowledge. Its chemistry is wonderful, and embraces all chemistry; its geography is equally so—its seas and rivers are even more wonderful than those of the earth; its temperature contains the whole theory of combustion. All knowledge, all taste, all sense of right and wrong, is comprehended within the sphere of the microcosm, man."

The correspondence between the individual man and the race is as complete in the moral realm as in the physical. The first state of man, as indicated in the Book of Genesis, was a condition of childhood. Its characteristic was simplicity and innocence. The people lived on the fruits of the earth and were familiar with the presence of their Creator, holding communion with him daily, as with a Father. With the increase of power resulting from development and growth, selfish desires began to be felt and yielded to, and the downward history was initiated. A knowledge of the distinction between good and evil can only come by the exercise of selfhood, which places the soul in opposition to God, who is the Source of all good.

The history of the fall is repeated in every human being. The child is born in a state of innocence. (The influence of heredity is not pertinent to this discussion.) The moment arrives when self-will is felt and asserted, and with this knowledge of good and evil begins the struggle of the two opposing principles for mastery.

It will thus be seen that evolution places the doctrine of man's fall upon a rational foundation. It coincides with and confirms the biblical account, if that account is taken spiritually; that is, not as a literal description, but as a history of the spiritual life of the race. The Bible teaches that man was first in a state of innocence. Satan tempted him with an appeal to his selfish nature, and he yielded and fell. Analogy shows the first innocent state to have been the childhood of the race. The scriptural record is merely an outline which evolution fills in and completes in accordance with God's universal laws.

EVOLUTION AND TOTAL DEPRAVITY.

The doctrine of "total depravity" has been regarded as one of the corner-stones of Calvinism, and at the same time it is one of the statements against which human nature is most strongly inclined to rebel. "No goodness in a human heart? No innocence in a new-born babe, fresh from the hand of the Divine Creator? Such a doctrine is incredible, monstrous. I have no use for a religion which proclaims it." Protests of this nature have always been roused by the dogma of total depravity as it has been stated.

Christian evolution solves the problem and reconciles the two opposing elements. It confirms the doctrine of human depravity, yet places it upon such a logical basis that all objection to it is dissolved and disappears.

The principle is a simple one. It may be presented in a series of postulates:

1. God is the Creator of all things, and the Source of all life.

2. He created matter and endowed it with all its "prom-

ise and potency." Its so-called laws are his methods of operation.

3. He creates all orders of animals, and imparts the life of each. Their life is his life in varied manifestations, according to the nature and quality of the receptacle that holds and uses it. The instinct of the ant, the bee, and the beaver, the intelligence of the dog, the horse, and the elephant, all are impartations of the divine life.

4. To man he imparts life in its highest form, giving it the impress of his own nature or image. But this introduces an element differing from all other manifestations of his life. It involves a power of choice, of acceptance, or rejection. Therefore man, unlike other forms of conscious life, holds his fate in his own hands.

5. The qualities which are lovely in a little child, because it is not responsible, become a savor of life unto life or of death unto death to the adult. Why? Because each quality must either be exercised for God or for self. The former is life. The latter is death. This is not the result of an arbitrary law, but is essential to the very nature of a moral and responsible being.

God's requirements are neither unjust nor unreasonable. "He knoweth our frame; he remembereth that we are dust." The standard he gave in the old dispensation was "to deal justly, to love mercy, to walk humbly before God." This is as true in heathen as in Christian lands, as plainly stated by St. Paul.

In the new dispensation, when the Son of God appeared upon the earth as the Saviour and instructor of the race, he announced the principle anew, explicitly and repeatedly stating that our love for God would be judged by our spirit and conduct toward our fellow-men.

The evolutionary theory of human depravity may be summed up in these words. Our capacities work for good or ill in proportion as they are or are not consecrated to God, that is, to our fellow-men. If they are not so consecrated they react upon themselves, the selfish principle becomes more and more confirmed, the soul drifts continually farther away from God, the only source of life. In this sense the self-nature is capable of becoming "totally depraved." All that is good in us, whether in childhood or at any later period of life, is from God. In proportion as we yield to the self-principle and thus withdraw from the Divine Source of life, of truth, and of love, our "depravity" or selfhood asserts its power and takes possession of us.

The theological statement of the doctrine has pressed it to an extreme. It has indicated human depravity as absolute, which every one who looks upon a little child knows cannot be true. The *capacity* for complete depravity or self-will is in the child, but the extent of its influence is a problem to be wrought out in the later history of each individual.

EVOLUTION AND FOREORDINATION.

Evolution *is* foreordination. It is God's way of foreordaining a race of beings for his eternal service and companionship. If we examine a bird we can read its history in its structure. Every portion of its being shows that it is foreordained to be an inhabitant of the air. Thus also with a fish. Every part of its structure, within and without, indicates its destiny. Its shape, its gills, its lungs, its fins—all point to the water as its proper home.

Examining in a similar way the spiritual nature of man, what qualities do we find which foreordain him to spend an eternity in hell?

Not one.

His faculties are reflections or finite reproductions of the divine. All his evils are perversions of gifts that in themselves are good. His pride is a perversion of a necessary self-respect, his wicked anger of a capacity for righteous indignation toward wrong, and thus with every vile and hurtful passion. A bird's wing may be maimed when young so that it is never able to soar into the element for which it was destined. Man has the power to maim his own soul so that he never reaches his predestined home. But that is his fault, and not God's. He is literally the Father of the entire human race, for he creates every member of it. None are orphans but those who refuse to accept his love and his life.

Foreordination, in the light of evolution, is the most intensely interesting and inspiring theme that can possibly engage our attention. It lifts our thoughts above the narrow limits of this small planet, and extends our view outward toward an infinite horizon. It asks a thousand questions, and points us to eternity for their answer. But in doing this it does not withdraw our attention from the small duties of daily life. On the contrary, it invests them with an unspeakable dignity by showing how they may serve as the seeds of an eternal harvest; buds from which heavenly flowers will bloom in the celestial gardens.

The doctrine of foreordination, when it is freed from the misleading definitions of a one-sided theology and is considered in the light of universal law, cannot but exercise a transforming influence upon the life and character. It leads us to study our various capacities and endowments for the purpose of discovering their latent possibilities. What eternal use is this or that gift foreordained by its nature to serve? What are these serious limitations in my character intended to accomplish for me or for others? Such questions, which are of deep concern to the thoughtful mind, even when considered only with reference to the brief span of our earthly existence, assume at once an infinite value and meaning when the view is projected forward into the boundless future.

He who receives and assimilates the truth that humanity is, by its divinely created faculties, fitted for an eternity of beneficent service, is raised above the power of low and unworthy thoughts. In their place he finds within his own being a spring of pure and perennial delight. Though within himself, he knows that this inspiration is not of himself. As the bubbling spring in the meadow has its source in the distant mountain heights, so does the recipient of this inward stir of inspiring thought recognize the divine origin of the sacred gift.

In reality, foreordination is simply the law of growth with an extension of the principle into the future world. The acorn is foreordained to be an oak, and it fulfils its destiny by obeying God's laws till the oak stands complete. Man has the power of resisting those laws to his own destruction. If it were possible for the young oak to refuse to receive the light and warmth of the sun, the result would only be a stoppage. It would cease to grow, the vital principle would depart, and the wood and leaves would return to earth again. But in man's nature there is an active principle which works ruin when left to itself. When he rejects God's light and heat—his truth and love

—this innate principle of selfishness takes possession of him, he sets himself against immutable law, and foreordains and accomplishes his own destruction.

EVOLUTION AND THE TRINITY.

The prevailing ideas among men concerning the Trinity were not derived directly from the Bible, but are the outgrowth of theological systems and metaphysical subtleties. Theology asserts the tripersonality of God, but the word "person" is not used in the Scriptures in relation to the Godhead. The Greek meaning of "person" is lost sight of. The false idea of a God of wrath necessitated a counterpart—a Saviour whose office should be to stand between a sinful race and a righteous God who cannot endure sin. Systematic theology begins by assuming or teaching that God is one, yet in the process of its instructions the impression of three distinct persons or beings is inevitable. Hence the idea as it exists in the minds of many, perhaps a majority of American Christians, is like this: that God the Father, self-existent, eternal, is the Creator and Preserver of the universe; that Jesus Christ the Son was created at a certain time to meet a certain exigency; that the Holy Spirit was sent after the mission of Christ was completed to carry on his work.

The sacred Scriptures give no ground for such confusion of thought except by sentences culled and selected to support a system. From first to last they proclaim the truth that God is one. "Hear, O Israel; the Lord thy God is one God." In the record of our Lord's life upon the earth this mistake appears to have been guarded against with special care. Nothing in all literature is more clear and unmistakable than the theological statements of John in the opening sentences of his Gospel: "In the beginning was the Word, and the Word was with God, and the Word was God."

In the law of evolution may be found a key to the mystery of three in one, or one including three. Starting with the truth of the unity of God, the principle of the Trinity can be clearly traced. Paul says with reference to the coming of the Messiah: "When the fulness of the time was come, God sent forth his Son." What constituted "the fulness of time"? What was the nature of the consummation that could be thus described? Obviously, it must have been that period in the development of the race when spiritual truth could be so received and assimilated as to create a new order of spiritual life. Christian evolution, although describing a gradual process, yet makes account of a series of distinct degrees. God created the cosmic dust and impressed it with certain laws or forces which led to the formation of our planetary system. After it was duly prepared, in "the fulness of time" he introduced the principle of organic life, and the world of vegetation came into being. The vegetable life developed from primitive forms to more finely wrought and complex organisms, and in "the fulness of time" conscious or animal life was evolved. The process of development still continued, pressing steadily upward to higher types, till in "the fulness of time" the moral element was introduced, and humanity was evolved with its self-conscious life and the power of choice and sense of responsibility which raised it to a condition of permanency or personal immortality.

As in the case of all the earlier epochs, the creation of humanity was but the beginning of a new order of development. The law of growth—the evolutionary process—was transferred from the body, which had reached the limit of its development, to the soul, whose history had just begun. During a period of unknown duration the work continued with many fluctuations till another consummation was attained. Humanity had so far risen in the moral scale of being that a new law of spiritual life could be received. The point was reached when in "the fulness of time" God himself could descend and become the Teacher of the race and the first-fruits of the new law—the law of self-sacrifice. But, like every other distinct epoch, the beginning was obscure and "without observation." Even the chosen people, who expected it and had anticipated it for centuries, failed to recognize the signs of its advent. "He came unto his own, but his own received him not." The infinite Jehovah, coming to this world "in the likeness of sinful flesh," planted the seeds of truth in an obscure corner of the world, and exemplified the truth by his life among a people who had no standing or influence in the great family of nations.

It will be seen that the evolutionary theory offers no temptation—in fact, it leaves no room—for any misleading views of distinct beings in the Godhead. It triumphantly confirms Christ's declaration "I and the Father are one," and Paul's statement "In him dwelleth all the fulness of the Godhead bodily." It is consistent with the great central truth of the gospel, "God so *loved* the world that he sent his only begotten Son." That there are difficulties in this theory does not affect the case. Any subject of infinite scope must present difficulties to the finite mind. But the apparent objections to this presentation are as nothing compared with the glaring inconsistencies of a "threefold Being." There is very little that is confusing in the thought of Christ as the human manifestation of God—a revelation of his eternal Fatherhood. When his redemptive work was finished, his infinite sacrifice completed, the third element of the Trinity, the Holy Spirit, moving upon the hearts of men, was but a further and permanent manifestation and exercise of God's love; the Father and the Son, the divine and the human, uniting in an active and energizing influence for elevating and perfecting the race.

Although the application of the evolutionary theory to Christ's coming and his work is not yet formally adopted in some schools of theology, its logical conclusions are widely accepted by progressive preachers and religious teachers. Professor Drummond says: "The incarnation is God making himself accessible to human thought." Dr. Phillips Brooks defines the Trinity in the following terms:

"1. God the Father, the creative deity;

"2. God the Son, the incarnate deity;

"3. God the Spirit, the infused deity, the manifestation of the divine energy."

The Lord's final commission to his followers was that they should go and make disciples of all the nations, "baptizing them into the name of the Father, and of the Son, and of the Holy Ghost." How did the Apostles interpret this command? Peter said at the close of his sermon on the day of Pentecost, "Repent ye, and be baptized every one of you *in the name of Jesus Christ.*" Some of the people of Samaria were afterward spoken of as having been "baptized into the name of the Lord Jesus." It is evident, therefore, that the early followers of Christ were not in the least confused or perplexed by any metaphysical distinctions with regard to the Trinity. They believed in one God. They accepted Jesus as an expression or manifestation of the divine: "God in Christ reconciling the world unto himself." They asked for no other creed, no other inspiration. In that power they went forth to win the nations of the earth.

The law of the Divine Trinity—three in one—is indicated by a thousand analogies in the world of nature. In fact, these correspondences are so numerous, so universal, that a review of them can lead to no other conclusion than that they must represent or express the very being of the Creator. Let us observe some of the illustrations:

The sun $\begin{Bmatrix} \text{heat} \\ \text{light} \end{Bmatrix}$ life.

The earth $\begin{Bmatrix} \text{air} \\ \text{earth} \end{Bmatrix}$ water.

Matter $\begin{Bmatrix} \text{gaseous} \\ \text{solid} \end{Bmatrix}$ fluid.

Creation $\begin{Bmatrix} \text{God} \\ \text{man} \end{Bmatrix}$ nature.

Kingdoms of nature $\begin{Bmatrix} \text{mineral} \\ \text{animal} \end{Bmatrix}$ vegetable.

The tree $\begin{Bmatrix} \text{roots} \\ \text{branches} \end{Bmatrix}$ trunk.

Architecture $\begin{Bmatrix} \text{right half} \\ \text{left half} \end{Bmatrix}$ keystone.

Harmony of color $\begin{Bmatrix} \text{blue} \\ \text{red} \end{Bmatrix}$ yellow.

Harmony of tones $\begin{Bmatrix} \text{the fifth} \\ \text{the first} \end{Bmatrix}$ the third.

Psychology $\begin{Bmatrix} \text{purpose} \\ \text{effect} \end{Bmatrix}$ means.

All knowledge $\begin{Bmatrix} \text{theology} \\ \text{science} \end{Bmatrix}$ philosophy.

It will be observed that in every case the third term has a peculiar relation to the other two. It is either a means of blending them or an outgrowth from them—sometimes both. To quote a few examples:

Theology treats of the great First Cause. Science treats of the results flowing from that Cause. Philosophy traces the connection between the two.

The first and fifth tones of the scale sounded together produce a dissonant effect. Introducing the third changes the dissonance to a perfect chord.

Red contrasted with blue produces a dissonance of color. Yellow blends them into perfect harmony.

The animal cannot subsist on the mineral. The vegetable assimilates the mineral and maintains the life of the animal.

Every expression of human life is a trinity of thought, feeling, and action.

All the trinities of nature are reflections of the Divine Trinity from which they spring.

$$\left.\begin{array}{l}\text{Love}\\ \text{Wisdom}\end{array}\right\} \text{power.}$$

God is three in One. Christ expresses Unity. He is the *Power* of God unto *Wisdom* (salvation) to all who are united to him by *Love*. The Father represents the divine. The Son represents the human, which he raises to the divine through self-sacrifice. The Holy Spirit is the divine life acting upon the hearts of men. Every object in the physical universe, being a combination of *substance*, *form*, and *use*, illustrates the " Trinity in Unity " of its Divine Creator.

EVOLUTION AND THE ATONEMENT.

The relation of evolution to the atonement is indicated by the definition of the Trinity previously given. The etymology of the word "at-one-ment" ought to have saved it from the perversions of a metaphysical scheme of salvation. But it did not, and one of the grandest practical results of the new presentation of the Divine Being as immanent in the universe will be to bring the world back to Christ's own definition of his work: "To preach the gospel to the poor; to heal the broken-hearted, to preach deliverance to the captives, and recovering of sight to the blind, to set at liberty them that are bruised."

It must not be inferred that evolution presents Christ only as a great Reformer. Every distinct stage in the evolutionary process teaches the necessity of a new birth. This is very clearly stated in Professor Drummond's well-known chapter on "Biogenesis": "Except a mineral be born 'from above'—from the kingdom just above it—it cannot enter the kingdom just above it. And except a man be born 'from above,' by the same law he cannot enter the kingdom just above him. This is not a dogma of theology, but a necessity of science."

For the purposes of this discussion little need be added to Professor Drummond's scientific interpretation of the doctrine. It shows the atonement to be a phase of God's eternal plan for creating and perfecting a race of immortal beings—a process in which the physical universe is only a starting-point. Every human being must become a partaker of the divine life in order to enjoy a blessed immortality. God seeks to impart this life to every one; in other words, to be "at one" with all who are made in his image. But the experience must be real, and it must be individual. The truth has been very clearly and vigorously expressed by Dr. George D. Herron as follows: "Christ is our righteousness, but not in any external sense; he is our righteousness, not in himself, but in ourselves. He is not our righteousness any more than we let him into the possession of our souls. And he cannot possess us from without. His sacrifice cannot take the place of our divine call to sacrifice. God will not accept his obedience as an apology for our disobedience; his love as the justification of our selfishness. Neither is his character a mere object-lesson—something for us to look at in spiritual wonderment, something to influence us by its objective power and beauty. Christ can be good in no man's stead; nor is there any imitation of Christ. His atonement is neither a legal nor a moral fiction. *The atonement is a reality.* It is the coming of God into humanity, a re-creation, a regeneration of the race from within. It is the indwelling of God in the soul. Hence, Christ is not our goodness any more than we allow him to make us good. He is not our Saviour any more than we trust him to make us like himself. As much of his righteousness is ours as we receive and work out in divine living, in Christly characters—no more."

THE TESTIMONY OF SCIENCE.

[NOTE.—Only those who have followed closely the recent revolution in the methods of discussing religious truth can fully realize the extent of the departure from the former modes of treatment. The radical change in the "point of view" is indicated by a remark of Dr. McCosh to his students, "A book now needs to be written bearing the same relation to evolution that Butler's 'Analogy' bore to the immature scientific knowledge of his day."

The basis of the new method of treatment has been so clearly and admirably stated by Professor John Fiske in his book "Excursions of an Evolutionist," that I am sure the reader will be grateful for the following somewhat extended quotation and also for the latest utterance of Professor Drummond.]

" If we look at all the systems or forms of religion of which we have any knowledge, we shall find that they differ in many superficial features. But amid all such surface differences we find throughout all known religions two points of substantial agreement. And these two points of agreement will be admitted by modern civilized men to be of far greater importance than the innumerable differences of detail. All religions agree in the two following assertions, one of which is of speculative and one of which is of ethical import. One of them serves to sustain and harmonize our thoughts about the world we live in and our place in that world; the other serves to uphold us in our efforts to do each what we can to make life more sweet, more full of goodness and beauty, than we find it. The first of these assertions is the proposition that the things and events of the world do not exist or occur blindly or irrelevantly, but that all, from the beginning to the end of time, and throughout the farthest sweep of illimitable space, are connected together as the orderly manifestations of a Divine Power, and that this Divine Power is something outside of ourselves, and upon it our own existence from moment to moment depends. The second of these assertions is the proposition that men ought to do certain things, and ought to refrain from doing certain other things, and that the reason why some things are wrong to do and other things are right to do is in some mysterious but very real way connected with the existence and nature of this Divine Power, which reveals itself in every great and every tiny thing, without which not a star courses in its mighty orbit, and not a sparrow falls to the ground. Matthew Arnold once summed up these two propositions very well, when he defined God as "an eternal Power, not ourselves, that makes for righteousness." This twofold assertion, that there is an eternal Power that is not ourselves, and that this Power makes for righteousness, is to be found, either in a rudimentary or in a highly developed state, in all known religions.

"Having thus seen what is meant by the essential truths of religion, it is very easy to see what the attitude of the doctrine of evolution is toward these essential truths. It asserts and reiterates them both; and it asserts them not as dogmas handed down to us by priestly tradition, not as mysterious intuitive convictions of which we can render no intelligible account to ourselves, but as scientific truths that have been disclosed by observation and reflection, like other scientific truths, and accordingly harmonize naturally and easily with the whole body of our knowledge. The doctrine of evolution asserts, as the widest and deepest truth which the study of nature can disclose to us, that there exists a Power to which no limit in time or space is conceivable, and that all the phenomena of the universe, whether they be what we call material or what we call spiritual phenomena, are manifestations of this infinite and eternal Power. Now, this assertion, which Mr. Spencer has so elaborately set forth as a scientific truth—nay, as the ultimate truth of science, as the truth upon which the whole structure of human knowledge philosophically rests —this assertion is identical with the assertion of an eternal Power, not ourselves, that forms the speculative basis of all religions. When Carlyle speaks of the universe as in very truth the star-domed city of God, and reminds us that through every crystal and through every grass-blade, but most through every living soul, the glory of a present God still beams, he means pretty much the same thing that Mr. Spencer means, save that he speaks with the language of poetry, with language colored by emotion, and not with the precise, formal, and colorless language of science. By many critics who forget that names are but the counters rather than the hard money of thought, objections have been raised to the use of such a phrase as the Unknowable whereby to describe the power that is manifested in every event of the universe. Yet when the Hebrew prophet declared that " by him were laid the foundations of the deep," but reminded us, " Who by searching can find him out?" he meant pretty much what Mr. Spencer means when he speaks of a Power that is inscrutable in itself, yet is revealed from moment to moment in every throb of the mighty rhythmic life of the universe.

"And this brings me to the last and most important point of all. What says the doctrine of evolution with regard to the ethical side of this twofold assertion that lies at the bottom of all religion? Though we cannot fathom the nature of the inscrutable Power that animates the world, we know, nevertheless, a great many things that it does. Does this eternal Power, then, work for righteousness? Is there a divine sanction for holiness and a divine condemnation for sin? Are the principles of right living really connected with the intimate constitution of the universe? If the answer of science to these questions be affirmative, then the agreement with religion is complete both on the speculative and on the practical sides; and that phantom which has been the abiding terror of timid and superficial minds—that phantom of the hostility between religion and science—is exorcised now and forever.

Now science began to return a decisively affirmative answer to such questions as these when it began with Mr. Spencer to explain moral beliefs and moral sentiments as products of evolution. For clearly, when you say of a moral belief or a moral sentiment that it is a product of evolution, you imply that it is something which the universe through untold ages has been laboring to bring forth, and you ascribe to it a value proportionate to the enormous effort that it has cost to produce it. Still more, when with Mr. Spencer we study the principles of right living as part and parcel of the whole doctrine of the development of life upon the earth; when we see that, in an ultimate analysis, that is right which tends to enhance fulness of life—we then see that the distinction between right and wrong is rooted in the deepest foundation of the universe; we see that the very same forces, subtle and exquisite and profound, which brought upon the scene the primal germs of life and caused them to unfold, which through countless ages of struggle and death have cherished the life that could live more perfectly, and destroyed the life that could only live less perfectly, until Humanity, with all its hopes and fears and aspirations, has come into being as the crown of all this stupendous work—we see that these very same subtle and exquisite forces have wrought into the very fibers of the universe those principles of right living which it is man's highest function to put into practice. The theoretical sanction thus given to right living is incomparably the most powerful that has ever been assigned in any philosophy of ethics. Human responsibility is made more strict and solemn than ever when the eternal Power that lives in every event of the universe is thus seen to be in the deepest possible sense the author of the moral law that should guide our lives."

As to the ethical side of the question—the "principles of right living" spoken of in the above quotation—most interesting and important testimony is given by Professor

Drummond in his volume on "The Ascent of Man." He claims that a vital mistake has been made in all discussions of evolution heretofore by accepting the struggle for life as the only controlling factor in development. "There is," he says, "a second factor, which one might venture to call the *struggle for the life of others*, which plays an equally prominent part. Even in the early stages of development its contribution is as real, while in the world's later progress—under the name of altruism—it assumes a sovereignty before which the earlier struggle sinks into insignificance. That this second form of struggle should all but have escaped the notice of evolutionists is the more unaccountable since it arises, like the first, out of those fundamental functions of living organisms which it is the business of biological science to investigate. The functions discharged by all living things, plant and animal, are two in number: the first is nutrition, the second is reproduction. The first is the basis of the struggle for life, the second, of the struggle for the life of others. One's first and natural association with the struggle for the life of others is with something done for posterity—in the plant the struggle to produce seeds, in the animal to beget young. But this is a preliminary which, compared with what directly and indirectly rises out of it, may be almost passed over. The significant note is ethical, the development of otherism as altruism—its immediate and inevitable outcome. Watch any higher animal at that most critical of all hours—for itself and for its species—the hour when it gives birth to another creature like itself. Pass over the purely physiological processes of birth; observe the behavior of the animal-mother in the presence of the new and helpless life which palpitates before her. There it lies trembling in the balance between life and death. Hunger tortures it; cold threatens it; danger besets it; its blind existence hangs by a thread. There is the opportunity of evolution. There is an opening appointed in the physical order for the introduction of a moral order. If there is more in nature than the selfish struggle for life, the secret can now be told. Hitherto the world belonged to the food-seeker, the self-seeker, the struggler for life, the father. Now is the hour of the mother. And, animal though she be, she rises to her task. And that hour, as she ministers to her young, becomes to her, and to the world, the hour of its holiest birth.

"Sympathy, tenderness, unselfishness, and the long list of virtues which make up altruism, are the direct outcome and essential accompaniment of the reproductive process. Without some rudimentary maternal solicitude for the egg in the humblest forms of life, or for the young among higher forms, the living world would not only suffer but would cease. For a time in the life-history of every higher animal the direct, personal, gratuitous, unrewarded help of another creature is a condition of existence. Even in the lowest world of plants the labors of maternity begin, and the animal kingdom closes with the creation of a class in which this function is perfected to its last conceivable expression. The vicarious principle is shot through and through the whole vast web of nature; and if one actor has played a mightier part than another in the drama of the past, it has been self-sacrifice. It is quite certain that, of all things that minister to the welfare and good of man, of all that make society solid and interesting, of all that make life beautiful and glad and worthy, by far the larger part has reached us through the activity of the struggle for the life of others.

"Evolution has ushered a new hope into the world. The supreme message of science to this age is that all nature is on the side of the man who tries to rise. Evolution, development, progress, are not only on her programme, these are her programme. For all things are rising, all worlds, all planets, all stars and suns. An ascending energy is in the universe, and the whole moves on with one mighty idea and anticipation. The aspiration in the human mind and heart is but the evolutionary tendency of the universe becoming conscious. Darwin's great discovery, or the discovery which he brought into prominence, is the same as Galileo's—that the world moves. The Italian prophet said it moves from west to east; the English philosopher said it moves from low to high. And this is the last and most splendid contribution of science to the faith of the world."

No, the concluding sentence must be amended. "The last and most splendid contribution of science to the faith of the world" has been made by Professor Drummond himself, in the basis which he has given for an ethical principle in evolution. The struggle for life has been aptly called "the Old Testament of evolution, with Darwin as its lawgiver, while the struggle for the life of others is the New Testament, with Professor Drummond as its evangelist."[1] Instead of the law, the gospel. Instead of selfishness, it is love which is "the supreme factor in the evolution of the world."

[1] *Review of Reviews*, July, 1894.

CHAPTER XXIV.

THE WAYS OF GOD IN THIS NEW AGE.

IN speaking of the ways of God in this new age it is not implied that he has changed, for this is impossible. There has been a great and marvelous change, but it is in us and not in him. It will be profitable to consider the governing characteristics of the present era, for the special purpose of determining how each of us may be so adjusted to the current of events as to do his work most thoroughly and effectively.

The first step to be taken is to establish in our minds the truth that this is God's world; that the ways of this marvelous era are his ways; and that the numberless forms of progress are simply the unfolding of his plan. Guizot, the French historian, says: " Man advances in the execution of a plan which he has not conceived, and of which he is not even aware. He is the free and intelligent artificer of a work which is not his own. Imagine a great machine the design of which is centered in a single mind, though its various parts are intrusted to different workmen, separated from and strangers to each other. No one of them understands the work as a whole, nor the general result which he concurs in producing; but every one executes with intelligence and freedom, by rational and voluntary acts, the particular task assigned to him."

We are such workmen, and the interest, enthusiasm, and efficiency of our work will depend largely upon our faith in the perfection of the plan, the wisdom of the Planner, and the degree of attention we regard him as giving to the execution of his great design.

God's ways in this new age may be considered under four heads: religion, social reforms, science, and education. Each of these topics demands a volume rather than a few paragraphs. Only the leading lines of thought can be suggested.

RELIGION.

The standards of religious life are being revolutionized. The truth is coming to be understood that intellectual assent to Christian doctrines does not, in itself, make a man a Christian, and that righteousness or uprightness cannot be transferred in a mechanical way, but must be received, assimilated, and manifested in a righteous life. Dr. W. R. Huntington says: "There is a growing disposition to regard the church of Christ as a training-school for souls in the process of saving, rather than as a museum of souls already saved." Dr. R. S. MacArthur writes as follows concerning the relation of this life to the future:

"Habit tends to fixity, and this fixity of habit becomes character. Character is the distinctive mark which thought and act make upon the soul. Character is the sum of qualities which make the man; character is the man. Character tends to become eternal. This is a solemn thought. There is a moral gravitation as truly as there is a natural gravitation. Like seeks like. In Acts iv. 23 we read of Peter and John, 'And being let go, they went to their own company.' Here is an illustration of a great law. Let a group of men loose on the confines of this life, and they will go to their own company. In Acts i. 25 it is said of Judas that he fell by transgression from his ministry and apostleship, 'that he might go to his own place.' Every man will go to his own place. Future punishment is not so much an external infliction as it is an inward condition. You cannot punish an innocent man; this the omnipotent God cannot do. Put a man who loves God anywhere, and he will have something of heaven; put a man who hates God anywhere, and he will have much of hell. Milton's Satan was right when he said, 'Which way I fly is hell; myself am hell.' God sends no man into perdition. The election of God is unto life; the election of death is voluntarily made by men. Analyze a man's deepest choices, and you can tell whither he is going. If he selects a course of life whose end is death, he selects hell as the inevitable goal of such a life. If a man persists in living in sin God cannot keep him out of perdition. When the end comes, that man goes downward as certainly as the man who loves God goes upward. God cannot, in harmony with his own laws of being, keep a man who loves him out of heaven. God is not arbitrary, fickle, and capricious. He will not violate the laws according to which he has created us."

George Macdonald states the case bluntly in a single sentence: "If any one thinks he can get to heaven because Christ died and not because of being righteous himself, he is a fool." Another writer states it thus: "Our characters, like our clothes, are spun thread by thread, and the finished garment will be exactly as we have made it."

SOCIAL REFORMS.

What power less than the Spirit of God could, in a single century, have changed so completely the attitude of the cultured classes toward the down-trodden millions of the race? Slaves, vassals, dependents—a lower order of creation born to minister to the luxury of the rich—such was the estimate in which the masses were held. Now there is no follower of the meek and lowly Jesus who dares entertain thoughts so degrading. A new word is upon men's lips—"altruism." The heaven-descended thought is abroad in the world, that our highest duty is to others and not to ourselves, and that through the performance of this duty our highest happiness will be attained.

> "Renounce joy for my fellow's sake? That's joy
> Beyond joy." [1]

The governmental policy of civilized nations is gradually becoming more humane, although the higher law of brotherhood is as yet far from being embodied either in the laws or the practice of so-called Christian governments. Legal enactments rarely have any higher purpose than the protection of our rights from infringement by that universal enemy, our fellow-man. Laws are an outgrowth of the average sentiment of the people who produce them. When a truly Christian nation is evolved we shall have a truly Christian jurisprudence. Daniel Webster had the clearness of vision to perceive and the courage to announce seventy years ago that there is no science of political economy. Why is this true? Because the present basis of political economy is selfishness or self-interest, and the principle of "every one for himself" can never be brought into form or order.

Until the present time the human race has had the spirit

[1] Browning.

of Cain and has sheltered itself behind the first murderer's arrogant and shameless question, "Am I my brother's keeper?" At last the world begins to realize the force of God's reply, "The voice of thy brother's blood crieth unto me from the ground." Of the countless forms of effort in behalf of universal justice which spring from our new sense of responsibility it is not within the scope of this brief discussion to speak.

Among the growing forces of the new age, the widening sphere of woman must be reckoned as by no means of least importance. While her influence has always been vital and beyond the possibility of measurement, yet it has been to a large extent latent, repressed; certainly it has been exercised but rarely in its fulness. Now, as ideas are everywhere broadening, and the principles which should govern society are being better understood, the absolute *need* of woman in every department of life is beginning to be recognized. There is a moral or spiritual side to every social question. Womanhood is peculiarly an expression or an embodiment of the moral and spiritual. Hence her influence is needed in a more direct and positive way than that of merely training her sons in the home. The problem of woman's part in the ideal social fabric is just beginning to be considered.

It is a remarkable ordering of Divine Providence, as if intended for an object-lesson at this particular time, that two individuals who are perhaps exerting the widest *personal* influence are women. Miss Frances E. Willard and Lady Henry Somerset are doing a work for the elevation of humanity which extends to the remotest corners of the earth, and they are doing this without sacrificing in any slightest degree the delicacy which belongs to the most refined womanhood. And in the realm of government, who stands higher in purity of personal life or shows a deeper sympathy with all broad measures for the welfare of mankind than Queen Victoria, the model queen and the model mother?

It is evident that the question of "woman's sphere" is rapidly settling itself.

SCIENCE.

The word "science" is here employed to indicate all forms of human knowledge. It is a glorious and inspiring truth that the development of human knowledge is now leading to a more profound knowledge of God. For a long time the revelations of science seemed to lead away from God. It was with the multitude as with the individual, a little knowledge was a dangerous thing. For many ages the investigations of the wisest men were all upon the surface. When they began to probe the deeper secrets of nature they at first struck the quicksands of doubt. That superficial stratum was soon passed, and an eternal foundation for faith has now been revealed in the principle of growth, or a progressive reception and expression of God. The more science the more faith. If this is not yet the invariable rule, it is rapidly becoming so. When Edison the inventor was asked the question, "Do you believe in an intelligent Creator, a personal God?" he replied, "Certainly. The existence of such a God can, to my mind, almost be proved by chemistry."

A practical engineer, Mr. Charles Talbot Porter, has written a book entitled "Mechanics and Faith," the purpose of which is to show that the fundamental principles of religion are proved by the laws of mechanics. His line of argument is as follows:

The laws of nature are modes of the divine activity. One who seeks to invent a new machine can do nothing by mere theory. He is obliged to appeal to the forces of nature, that is, to God. The Bible and nature both represent God as a Being of infinite and unchangeable truth. As the Bible enjoins obedience, so do the laws of the physical world. Three phenomena are apparent in nature: force, choice (elective affinity), and uniformity of action. As each of these contributes to some ultimate result, they afford unmistakable evidence of an underlying purpose. There can be no purpose without a Being to conceive and execute it. The presence and activity of an infinite God therefore appears as a demonstrated truth.

Such is the testimony of science at the close of the nineteenth century.

EDUCATION.

The fourth topic, education, really includes all the others. The predominating characteristic of the new age may be summed up in the single word, education. Religion is education. Social life is education. Science is education. That one word, in its broadest sense, covers all that distinguishes man from the anthropoidal ape. If eating and drinking and enjoyment of the pleasures of this world is our standard, we might as well be monkeys living in trees as human beings dwelling in palaces. "Oh, the pity of those lives that are taken up with the things which perish with the using!" exclaims Mrs. Alice Freeman Palmer, speaking from the depth of her noble womanhood.

God's dealings with mankind have always been of an educative nature. In the case of the Israelites, who were dealt with in a special and peculiar manner, we see the very perfection of an educational process. During the forty years of their wanderings in the wilderness they were subject to rigid military training. In fact, that may be described as the first military school, with God as the teacher. They were transformed in a single generation from a horde of slaves to a well-disciplined army and a well-ordered nation.

In a less marked but no less effective way the wisdom of the Great Educator can be seen in the development of mankind since that time. God has sent "beacon lights" in all ages of history to set before the race a higher ideal, to point to a nobler destiny in the future. Such were Plato, Aristotle, Socrates, and other leaders of thought in the past.

The providential instruments for inaugurating the later and higher, because more spiritual, era of education were the following: Lord Bacon introduced the inductive method and philosophy; Comenius taught its application to the child; Pestalozzi led the way in reducing the theory to practice; Froebel placed it upon an eternal foundation by showing that right education includes the development of the entire being, and that its end is nothing less than "to unite the soul to God." In announcing this truth and in showing how it can be philosophically applied, Froebel gave a stamp of sanity to all educational principles, and brought the beginnings of heavenly order into this chaotic world.

The result is scarcely felt as yet. The first effect of a dawning sense of justice in the popular mind is not to bring peace, but strife. The impulse of the undisciplined multitude under the influence of a dim perception of the normal relationship which should exist between man and his fellow-man is to meet wrong with wrong. But this is only a stage of growth. It is the beginning of a glorious end. Right is might. God is in his world. Truth will conquer falsehood. Love will master hate. The sociological problems which confront us in this new age are most complex, and in some of their aspects appalling. But they are a prophecy of their own solution. At this time of strikes and anarchism we sometimes think we have fallen upon evil days. The evil days were those in which there were no such problems. Now that justice—which is but a form of love—is recognized as an essential element in the "science of society," we may be sure that the consummation of the ages is approaching. This truth is a trumpet-call to every earnest soul. Dr. Josiah Strong has put the case clearly in the closing paragraphs of his admirable book, "The New Era; or, the Coming Kingdom":

" God has immense interest in this world, and an immense work to do here, and, as an old proverb says, ' God loves to be helped.' The best way to serve him that I know of is to help him do his work; that is, to help him perfect humanity, and thus to hasten the coming of his kingdom. Christ teaches that the needs of men are *his* needs; that he is in the world, hungry, naked, sick, in prison. If we wish to serve him, how can we do it better than in the person of those with whom he identifies himself? Self-giving is the law of Christian living; but self-sacrifice for its own sake is not good, and is no more pleasing to God than to human nature. To teach that God requires it or is pleased by it is to caricature him. But self-denial *for the sake of others* is Christ-like, God-like. When a man has what Clement of Rome called 'an insatiable desire for doing good' it makes sacrifice not only easy but blessed.

"The Captain of our salvation summons his church militant to-day, not to a forlorn hope, but to certain and glorious victory. Oh that the whole church with unbroken line might spring forward to offer the *living* sacrifice, until the kingdom is fully come, and God's will is done on earth even as it is in heaven!"

But in order to give largely we must first receive largely. One of the grandest characteristics of this new age is a clearer understanding and a fuller reception of the truth that we can "do all things through Christ." He came that we might have life, and that we might have it abundantly. The height, depth, and breadth of this truth has been largely lost sight of since the first centuries. It is a lesson which needs to be learned afresh. Life, health, strength, courage, unlimited ability to achieve—all this has been God's promise from the earliest dispensations to all who would go forward in faith. Christ came not to destroy the law, but to fulfil it. "The glory of Christianity is not to be as unlike other religions as possible, but to be their perfection and fulfilment."[1]

When the truths of Christ are spiritually discerned they are seen to be of absolutely unlimited application. "I am come that ye may have life, and that ye may have it abundantly," does not mean that we may only have an abundance of a certain kind of religious experience. It means that health may be ours—health of soul and health of body to the fullest extent that our faith will receive it.

[1] Dr. Jowett.

The supply is always equal to the demand. Emerson said: "There is but one Mind, and each human being is a different expression of it." We express all of the divine that we have faith to receive. "It is not enough to do our best, we must do better than our best." This is a wise injunction, for it implies that when we do our best something higher and nobler will be added to it. Paul speaks of the redemption of the body, but this truth has been totally ignored by most religious teachers. The doctrine is now coming to the front once more. Dr. George D. Herron says: "The redemption of the body will be one of the issues of our faith in Christ. . . . When the life of man becomes a harmony with God, sickness will be among the old things that have passed away. Implicit obedience to the will of God that was in Christ would abolish disease in three generations. When the law of love is perfectly obeyed on earth, the curtain of heaven shall be lifted and the mystery and grief of death shall be taken away; men will die as the rosebud dies when the rose blooms. The earthly and heavenly life will move in eternal unity, men not knowing one from the other. The perfection of our faith in Christ will be the perfection of our bodies in him."

Mr. Henry Wood, author of "The Political Economy of Natural Law," amplifies this truth in his volume, "Ideal Suggestions." Treating of the body, he quotes the couplet:

"For of the soul the body form doth take,
For soul is form, and doth the body make."

He then says:

"The human body is a holy temple. The external sanctuary of the soul, unlike temples made with hands, is built from within. It is the acme of God's material handiwork, the masterpiece of the Divine Architect. The living statue is modeled and draped with transcendent delicacy, grace, and symmetry. It is a cosmos in miniature, an epitome of the natural universe. Robing, as it does, the offspring of the Infinite, it is hallowed and sanctified. The breath of God gently swept through its aisles and corridors, and dedicated it as his own cathedral. Its walls and towers are built of living stones. Something has been taken from every known substance and blended in beautiful and harmonious proportion to form the finished structure. From its deep recesses the aortal organ sends out its rhythmical energy, which penetrates every highway and byway to the utmost limits. Its drum-beat never tires, and its measured pulsation is unceasing. Five temple gates open outward into highways which extend to the world of form, and through them messages are going and coming in endless succession.

"The body is a superlative example of coöperation—a general partnership where each member holds a unique office. Each unceasingly works not so much for itself as for all the others. Each one is an example of altruistic energy and ministry. Every tissue and molecule is on the alert, and its part is promptly and intelligently performed. All are good, for each is divinely perfect, and therefore the various offices of the members are alike honorable. Any seeming dishonor is only an abuse and degradation of that which received Christly consecration. Says Paul in his letter to the Romans, 'Nothing is unclean of itself: save to him who accounteth anything to be unclean, to him it is unclean.' All God's creations are good, and all impurity exists only in the perverted human consciousness. This beautiful and perfect instrument is the ideal human body, untouched by abnormity.

"But turning from the normal and ideal to actualized expression, we find the instrument discordant and unreliable. Instead of exercising sweet ministry, it at length demands to be constantly pampered and indulged. It insists upon much consideration, flattery, and idolizing, and finally mounts the throne as a capricious monarch. It compels homage, refuses to render reasonable coöperation, and, if its sway continues, finally destroys all harmony and revels in discord.

"God made man a 'living soul,' and therefore he *is* a soul, not *has* a soul. His body is a temporary material correspondence—a set of instruments for his convenience on the plane of sense. Through their use the real man—who can never be seen or heard—translates and manifests himself. . . .

"Love is the great healing power of the universe. We are miserable because we are full of conscious and unconscious antagonisms, and believe that 'things are against us.' On the contrary, every real force in existence is friendly. Whenever we send out loving thought in generous profusion, every part of our environment echoes back a sweet benediction. Even seeming enemies, personal and impersonal, are no exception. Love invigorates. Its electric thrill sends new life through sluggish minds, weak bodies, and paralyzed limbs. At the beautiful temple gate Peter and John concentrated such a current of healing love upon the lame man that he at once walked, leaped, and praised God. That wonderful power has never been withdrawn from the world, for *God never takes back;* and it only needs the same kind of consecration and positive spiritual clearness in some modern Peter and John for like manifestations now. Love is the great universal spiritual law of attraction which binds God and all his creatures unto harmonious unity, wipes away all tears, and heals all seeming infelicities."

Dr. W. H. Holcombe has epitomized much truth in a few sentences:

"Every man is a thought of God—a form of the Divine Truth, born of the Father or the Divine Love, and destined by appointed ways to work out and ultimate the divine purposes. This is the true doctrine of predestination and of immortality.

"Truth is God thinking in us. Goodness is God feeling in us. All our movements from goodness and truth are God working through us. And yet we are not God, nor is this pantheism. It is the Christian's union with God. *That they all may be one: as thou, Father, art in me and I in thee, that they may also be one in us—I in them and thou in me.*

"Although our life is strictly God's life, he permits us to feel it as our own, and to use it as our own. It therefore becomes finited, or made human in us. This is the origin of free agency. There are two factors in every case —God's will and man's will. So far as we are in God and in the order of his creation and providence our life is real; good, wise, beautiful, happy, each in his sphere and place."

By the voice of many witnesses these great biblical and eternal truths are being established in the world.

The guiding principles of the new dispensation may be summed up as follows:

1. The supernatural and the natural are one.

2. The spiritual is the only real.

3. All things are sacred, and "every common bush afire with God."

4. Human strength is divine strength received and individualized through the power of choice.

5. Through the power of choice heaven or hell is created in our own souls. Of the heavenly kingdom, Jesus Christ is the chief corner-stone. The rule of life is exceedingly simple. "*Let* this mind be in you which was also in Christ Jesus." "*Let* your light so shine." By obeying this injunction we become recipients and ministers of the very life of God, and "neither death nor life, nor angels, nor principalities, nor powers, nor things present, nor things to come, nor height, nor depth, nor any other creature, shall be able to separate us from the love of God which is in Christ Jesus our Lord."

UNIVERSAL SONG.

ALTHOUGH all people are enjoined in the Sacred Scriptures to sing God's praises, yet the ability to obey the injunction is limited to a small number. The discovery has been made in England that the limitation is not necessary, as it grows out of the complexities of the method by which music has heretofore been taught. There is a *natural* method, called the Tonic Sol-fa system, which makes the reading of music as simple and easy as the reading of English. The popular music of England has been transformed by this method. In many cities and villages the great oratorios are sung by artisans and working people with as much ease as a plain church tune is sung in America.

Further information concerning the Tonic Sol-fa system can be obtained by sending ten cents for a pamphlet by Theodore F. Seward entitled "A Revolution in Music Teaching." Address

THE BIGLOW & MAIN CO.,
76 East Ninth Street,
New York.

THE BROTHERHOOD OF CHRISTIAN UNITY.

THE Brotherhood of Christian Unity is not an organization. It is a spirit. Recognizing the fact that Christendom is not yet prepared for a complete and final organic union of its various divisions, the Brotherhood seeks to do all in its power to lead up to and hasten the final consummation. The work of to-day is chiefly educational and preparative. One element of preparation is supplying a formula upon which all can agree, including those who are not ready to accept the creeds of the churches. This is supplied by the Brotherhood as follows: *For the purpose of uniting with all who desire to serve God and their fellowmen under the inspiration of the life and teachings of Jesus Christ, I hereby enroll myself as a member of the Brotherhood of Christian Unity.*

The following are among the specific aims of the Brotherhood:

1. To encourage the union of the various Christian bodies.

2. To aid every form of coöperative work for the welfare of mankind.

3. To distribute literature tending to unity.

4. To advocate the universal observance of the Christian year as a means of fixing attention upon the life and work of Jesus Christ, and thus avoiding contention over theories about him.

Those who desire cards of enrollment or further information about the Brotherhood may address (with stamp)

THEODORE F. SEWARD,
East Orange, New Jersey,
U. S. A.